THE
RAMPARTS WE GUARD

By R. M. MacIver

TOWARDS AN ABIDING PEACE

THE WEB OF GOVERNMENT

THE MORE PERFECT UNION

THE RAMPARTS WE GUARD

THE
RAMPARTS WE GUARD

R. M. MacIVER

THE MACMILLAN COMPANY

New York · 1950

NOTE

This book contains, with some expansion, the substance of the Weil Lectures delivered by the author before the University of North Carolina, in March, 1949. The author takes the opportunity to express his gratitude to the company of scholars at that University who gave him so cordial and hospitable a welcome; and especially to then President Frank Graham, now Senator Graham, and to Professors Howard W. Odum, Gordon W. Blackwell, C. B. Robson, and Harold Hotelling. I am much indebted to Dr. Herbert Deane for his careful scrutiny of the text and for the Index, and to my wife for undertaking the task of proofreading in my absence.

R. M. MacIver

CONTENTS

Part One

———•—

THE FAILURE TO UNDERSTAND

Chapter One

———•————

OUR NEGLECTED HERITAGE

We would all agree that to possess a precious thing and yet to be careless about what it is, to be ignorant of what it is, to take no well-considered steps to guard this thing, to entertain shallow and sometimes foolish ideas about it, would be a case of lamentable folly. That, nevertheless, is what we commonly do about a very precious thing, something indeed beyond price, something that sustains and enriches the very substance of our lives, something that has the greatest and most enduring benefits to confer, first on ourselves and then on all the world. We confuse it with other things. We do not even perceive the dangers that threaten to despoil it. This thing is our heritage of democracy.

The very fact that it is a heritage, that we are born into it, that it has become our portion without struggle and travail on our part, dims our perception of it. It was won through centuries of daring and stubborn conflict against entrenched power and privilege, against all the indoctrinations of those who held the keys of church and state. Those who won it were sustained by a great faith and a great vision. Only by great faith could it be won. Only by faith can it be kept. We keep it not as a tradition merely, for thus it loses its meaning for the present and turns into a superstition. It must live *in* us, forever newly responsive to the changing times.

The future of human society depends on how well we guard

this thing. It cannot be guarded by armies and navies. What they can do is to defend at need its true guardians. Its true guardians are the people themselves. It cannot be protected by laws against violators. It is not protected by the Constitution, which is but a first blueprint of the possession we now own. There is only one way to keep it in being, and that is through the intelligent perception, permeating the people, of what it is and of what makes it precious. We guard our spiritual treasures only by learning to appreciate them.

One curious aspect of our negligence is that there are very few books to which we can turn, and particularly few by Americans, that seriously try to enlighten us about the nature of democracy. If on the contrary we want expositions of the nature of dictatorship we can find them a-plenty. Thousands of books have been written about its various forms. Its philosophy, its structure, its goals, have been and are being expounded without end by those who subscribe to its principles. But you will find a scant handful of books that offer enlightenment on the principle of democracy. We seem so ready to take democracy for granted, to regard it as self-explanatory. There are indeed books that sing its praises, as there are books that damn it, but there are very few that genuinely study it and interpret it. The man in the street thinks democracy a simple thing that needs no comprehension, and it would almost appear as if the political scientist thought likewise. It is the "rule of the people," and the people rule by pulling down at certain intervals the levers of the voting machine.

But democracy is a rich and complex thing, much less simple in its actuality and in its significance than are the systems that oppose it. When we think it needs no understanding we are most apt to misunderstand it. Democracy is the living changing fabric of a slowly emergent way of conducting the government of men. All other systems need no long gestation to be born. They are maintained by far ruder, more elementary processes and methods. The people who live under them do not need to understand them—all they need to do is to obey. When they are "explained" to the people it is in order that the people may the more readily obey, not that they may be enabled the better to carry on the business of government. Under other systems the people must be passive to the will of government. Under democracy they must actively participate in the making of that will.

And yet this flexible and finer and more difficult scheme called democracy is not deemed to need or to deserve the patient, faithful exercise of the intelligence we apply to so many things that matter to us much less. It is true we have numbers of studies on how the Congress is organized and how its committees function, on the division of rights and powers between the Federal Government and the states, on the historical details of the administration of particular governments, on the changing balance of the party system, and so forth. But all these things assume the quality of democracy. They throw sidelights on its operation but they do not explain its nature. Democracy has its reporters and its orators, but where are its philosophers and its sages?

Every government rests on the acquiescence or the goodwill or the active consent of the governed. All other governments require the disciplined acceptance, the unquestioning obedience, of subjects. Democracy requires the enlightened partnership of citizens. Every system of government has its appropriate philosophy, without the widespread inculcation of which it can make no effective stand against the forces of disruption. Democracy has been negligent in articulating its philosophy. It has not realized how much its strength, its very life, depends on the citizens' perception of its nature, on the unity of spirit that grows out of the animated recognition of its values. We have been lax in this regard. We have failed to see, for example, how certain behavior on the part of citizens or of government flagrantly contradicts and corrupts and weakens both the principles we profess and the morale we need.

The evidence is damning enough. The capital of the United States, with all its memorials dedicated to liberty, maintains a policy of Negro exclusion, in housing, in the schools, in most forms of business, in hospitals, and in churches. Thus we disarm ourselves when we appear before the nations as the champions of civil rights. Often we do not even surmise that our actions betray our goals. In Nuremberg and in Tokyo we set up tribunals in the name of "international law," professing to vindicate democratic ideas of justice. We had no warrant of any kind to arrogate to ourselves, and to our allies, the exclusive right to administer international law. We had no international law to administer. The conquerors brought the conquered to the judgment seat and they condemned the conquered under the form of democratic legal procedure. The only right the conquerors had was the "right" of power. The denial of that "right" is a fundamental principle of democracy. The guilt of the condemned may have been black as night. That is not the issue. The guilty could have been dealt with as the victors pleased, but when the latter pretended to set up tribunals of "international law" legally entitled to try the accused, they were mocking the principles of justice and when they condemned the accused under this process they came dangerously near to the guilt of "judicial murder."

Always, in a democracy, both citizens and leaders are under obligation to comprehend its principles. In the second case we mentioned it is the leaders who were mainly responsible. In the first case it is mainly the body of citizens, the business men, the churchmen, the real estate agents, the well-to-do, the members of trade unions, and so forth, though a particular group of legislators has actively fostered the prevailing anti-democratic prejudice. Through lack of comprehension many of our people are quite unaware of the injuries they do to the democracy they believe in. And a sizable group of legislators—senators and congressmen—are so blind to democratic principles, so prejudiced, that in caucus and in committee they seek to frustrate and to curtail some of the elementary liberties on which democracy depends. The need for comprehension is intensified in our own time. There are stronger challenges from without—which here and there receive sympathetic resonance from within—and there is also disintegration within. There are forces of change to meet which we need a reassertion of the principle of democracy, a revindication of its worth, a reapplication of its values. We cannot cling to antique expressions and outmoded embodiments of the principle. The only way we can keep our spiritual inheritance, whether democracy or any other of the enduring values that man has attained in age-long strivings, is to translate them anew into the language and into the institutions of our own time, to apprehend their meaning for the present. Our "eternal values" die if in our reverence for the past we cling to the formulas of other days. The formulas must pass if the values they incorporated are themselves to endure.

There is another reason why the understanding of democracy is essential for Americans of our time. We are no longer only a nation among the nations. We are emphatically no longer a nation insulated from the other nations. If we are challenged we are also emulated. As a world power we cannot help influencing the whole world. By us the other democracies of the world are sustained. On us the non-democracies look with wary and often envious eyes. The world repute of democracy hangs on *our* democratic achievements. But if we fail to understand we fail also to achieve. In this storm-shadowed world we need a clear sense of direction. Beyond the issues of every day, to redeem the disputes and vexations and self-centered interests of the political struggle, we need the warm light of a guiding principle, the sense of a goal toward which we move. The goal is a principle of life, by following which the quality of man is vindicated and fulfilled. What has democracy to contribute to that end? Unless we can answer our power is spent in vain.

Unless we can answer we have no dynamic as a people and thus no unity. There is no national achievement without the perception of great enduring purpose, and when the purpose lags the achievement fades. It has been so with the great peoples of the past. Unless they had a contribution to make to humanity their mere power dissipated itself in ruinous contention or in the lust for possession. So it has been with Athens and Rome, with the empires of the East, with Carthage, with Genoa and Venice, with modern Germany. Power and pride and glory will never unite us any more. Our resources are greater than those of any other nation past or present. But when we say *ours,* who are we? They are not *our* resources unless we are one people, united by a unifying intrinsic purpose, not the extrinsic aim of domination. Otherwise our strength will break into the rival resources of embattled groups among us and of soulless dominating corporations and of ambitious seekers after greater wealth and power. If the United States does not exist as the embodiment of a clear democratic goal, it does not exist at all. It is only a congeries of men, a mechanism, a loose array of narrow-thoughted organizations.

When we fail to realize the meaning, the significance, of democracy we forsake both our heritage and our future. We are, it is true, more than a democracy, but democracy is the condition of our nationhood and the vehicle through which we can attain the fuller national being that is the expression of our capacity and ingenuity and many-sided humanity.

In the chapters that follow the attention of the reader is directed to certain major perils that confront us and threaten our unity. They threaten our unity because they confound both our understanding of the meaning of democracy and our adherence to the principle of democracy. If we perceive the nature of these perils we may at the same time quicken and enlarge our understanding of what democracy means in our present world. Two tasks of political interpretation are of moment to us in this new stage of our history. One is the interpretation of the essential character of democracy itself, democracy as one of the two opposing principles by resort to which men can be governed, democracy in all its forms as a contender against the opposing principle in all its forms, democracy as a world force, democracy as an embracing system of which we and other peoples are the heirs and guardians. The other task is the more intimate study of one kind of democracy, our own peculiar kind, with its particular inheritance, with its particular distribution of the responsibilities and functions of government, with its particular difficulties, with its particular genius. It is with the first of these two tasks we shall mainly be concerned, with only occasional consideration of the other.

The perils of democracy arise from several sources. One peril springs from the sheer misunderstanding of what it means. Another proceeds from the unwillingness of men and groups to face its demands when these demands are opposed to their prejudices, their traditions, or their interests. Such men and groups "accept" democracy, they profess to be its supporters, but actually they do what they can to undermine it. The maintenance of democracy requires the observance of certain ethical standards on the part of rulers and of citizens. It requires, for example, that every person be publicly treated as a person, not as a member of a class, group, or race, that his civil rights be not limited on irrelevant grounds, that is, on grounds other than his own violation of the civil rights of other men. Such ethical standards distinguish democracy from other forms of government. To deny them is to deny democracy. Yet this denial is frequently made by the citizens of our democracy and sometimes by our rulers and judges. On occasion the Supreme Court of the United States, under the guise of judicial review, has taken a stand against democracy, as when it declared invalid the Civil Rights Act of 1875. Happily, however, it later reversed its stand and became on the whole the guardian of our democracy. But our history provides sufficient instances to show how easy it is for the citizens and the statesmen of a democratic state to betray the requirements of their democracy.

Another peril arises from the concentration of power, tempting the strong to exploit the weak. Power of any sort, economic power, the power that is vested in the heads of any organization, whether it be an industrial or financial corporation, a church, an educational system, a trade union, or any other, tends to separate men from their less powerful fellows and thus to reduce the range of their sympathies. Power tends to engender assumptions of superiority that only very wise men can hold in check. If not thus checked the exercise of power weakens the sense of community, corrupts the perception of the greater common good. Power then becomes vain and hard-shelled and anti-democratic. Since economic power has so vast a range of operation and since it is now consolidated in such massive organizations constant vigilance is needed to counteract the peril thus created for democracy. In times of trouble particularly, economic power is likely to take sides with the anti-democratic forces.

An allied peril arises from the rivalries and ambitions of dominant groups, in which they become obsessed by their dividing interests and disregard the common good. The working of a democratic system requires that the common good be safeguarded against the organized ambitions and propagandistic drives of competing groups, which set their own advantage against the welfare of the whole and seek to make government the agency of their adventures for wealth and for power. It is the principle of democracy that all men are equally citizens, and the presumption back of this is the presence of a common interest that is indivisibly the concern of all citizens and that is greater and more worthwhile than the interests dividing them.

Another peril arises from our failure to reapply our democratic principles to changing conditions and changing needs. This peril becomes particularly serious in times of crisis or of rapid socio-economic change. We may, for example, falsely identify democracy with an established economic order and when that happens we are often ready to defend this order by resorting to undemocratic procedures. Or, on the other hand, we may be so convinced of the desirability of a new or reformed economic order that we are minded to abandon democratic liberties altogether in order to bring it about. We may even be so misguided, or so unscrupulous, that we claim thereby to be setting up a new and far superior kind of "democracy." In the clashes and crises that come from the champions of opposite economic systems the very being of democracy may be destroyed. Extremist demands, which impatiently reject the democratic necessity for the ripening of public opinion, are likely to arouse equal impatience in the opposing forces. Between the two the spirit of democracy can find no place. It was so in the young democracies of Europe after the First World War. It was so in Germany during the Weimar regime, when a threatening Nazism contended with a threatening communism. It was so in Spain when the extremists of the left contended against the reactionary forces of the old order. It has happened many times and it may be happening to-day. There is danger that it may happen in so long established a democracy as that of France. The outcome of the clash of opposites is the end of democracy, the victory of fascism or of left-wing totalitarianism.

Such clashes reveal another source of danger to democracy, to which we shall give particular attention. Other forms of government are unified from above. Authority is not derived from the people but imposed on them and strengthened by all the monopolistic indoctrination that an undisputed authority can engineer. The solidarity of other forms of government depends on the prestige and power of that over-all authority. But the solidarity of a democracy is the solidarity of the people themselves. The government is their government. Its unity and its strength is *their* unity and the strength of *their* common will to maintain it, of *their* common belief in its value. In our own times forces are at work to break up the sense of community, of the common weal, the union one and indivisible of the citizens of a democracy. The continuous disturbance of rapid social change, the growth of specialization and the ever more elaborate organization of specialized groups, each with its own detached interests, the consequent loss of universal folkways, the proliferation of creeds and ideologies each challenging the others—all these characteristics of our modern civilization have adverse influences on the solidarity of democratic peoples. Democracy cannot live merely in the "balance of interests," it must reassert the inclusive interest. It must rediscover its own solidarity and thus find new authority and new inspiration in its own intrinsic worth.

Chapter Two

———•———

LIBERTY, EQUALITY, AND FRATERNITY

The first and most insidious threat to democracy comes from false conceptions of what it is, of what it *means*. We are so familiar with democracy that we often think its meaning is too plain to need any examination. But familiarity may breed misunderstanding, here as elsewhere. We fail to see the importance of the things we take for granted. We may spring to their defense when they are manifestly threatened. We may have an inkling of what the loss of them would mean. But we still have no conception of the positive nature or the worth or the service of the thing we dread to lose. So it is with our attitude to democracy.

In our time, when democracy is subject to new and formidable challenge, we run great risks because of our lack of understanding of what it means. The devotees of opposing systems take advantage of our complaisance, of our ignorance concerning what is ours. Sometimes, to deceive us or to deceive their own people, they themselves assume the mask and the name of democracy. They seek thus to mislead us and to gain their own ends. The people of the United States have now the mission to comprehend their democracy, to defend it at home, and to implement the pledges their statesmen have made in its name. For example, they were pledged at Yalta to solve the pressing problems of European reconstruction by "democratic means." The same pledge was given by democratic England and by undemocratic Soviet Russia. The last-named power has persistently twisted the meaning of that pledge, putting a construction on the word "democracy" that is violently opposed to all past usage and to the whole line of historical development. How can we meet such claims, how can we live up to our pledges as a great world-power, how can we maintain any sense of national integrity, unless we have a clear understanding of the significance of the democratic premises on which our system of government rests?

The first need is that we rid ourselves of confused notions. The words we use to express the essentials of democracy are heavy with misleading overtones. The French Revolution proclaimed the inauguration of democracy as the reign of liberty, equality, and fraternity. The words had a wonderful resonance to those who were seeking deliverance from the oppressiveness, spoliation, and insolent pride of the oligarchical class-bound state. They conveyed the happiest sense of a new and better world. Of the three words, "fraternity" alone was free from ambiguities. Fraternity, with its injunction that men should regard their fellow men as brethren, across all boundaries, across all distinctions of people and race, across all differences of station and power, expressed a principle very congenial to the substance of democracy. But the other two words, for all their splendid appeal, threw their light to distant peaks and hid the treacherous ground that lay between. And before the Revolution ended, in the terror and confusion that led to Napoleonic Caesarism, the more thoughtful had begun to learn to be wary of acclaiming noble absolutes as direction signs pointing toward the democratic state.

In the first place there are many kinds of liberty and many kinds of equality. Some liberties are hard to reconcile with others, and some are totally obnoxious to others. Some kinds of equality are at war with others, some kinds are incompatible with any social order and some in particular are incompatible with democracy. When Liberty and Equality are worshipped as goddesses they lead the confused worshippers to chaos.

The confusion of democracy and equality has been baneful in the past, and still is common among us. Democracy confers certain rights *equally* on all men—it does not do the impossible, make them equal in skill or intelligence or position or power or influence or authority. In none of these respects are men ever equal nor can any kind of government ever make them equal. Let us observe that equality by itself is no ideal thing. If all men were equally wretched, equally poor, or equally powerful, the equality would be no boon. In a menagerie all the animals are equally under the whip. In a slave state all men, except the slave-drivers, are equal in servitude. In this sense men may be more equal under a totalitarian regime than under a democracy. Sometimes the oppressed cry out for equality when they mean instead liberation from their oppressors. Men who are free from oppression and exploitation do not raise the flag of equality. If men say they want to be free and equal their demand for freedom puts a limit on their demand for equality. Democracy, by assuring men of fundamental rights, makes them equal thereby in respect of the exercise of these rights. They are equal before the law, they are equal as citizens, equal as voting units, equally free to speak their minds and to organize in the pursuit of their interests.

Democracy bestows on all citizens fundamental rights. It is claimed that they cannot effectively exercise these rights unless they are equal in all other respects as well, that liberty and equality are the two sides of the same shield. The claim is justified *up to a point.* The danger comes when no heed is paid to the question of limits. It is dangerous to say loosely, as does Harold Laski, that "the more equality there is in a State the more use, in general, we can make of our freedom." Beyond certain limits equality and liberty are opposed. Although Laski denies it, Lord Acton was right in saying that in the time of the French Revolution the passion for equality made vain the hope of freedom. Any attempt to achieve equality in wealth for all citizens would surely result in the most extreme totalitarianism. To keep men equal in wealth, in spite of their unequal abilities and varying aptitudes, would require a degree of all-round regimentation vastly surpassing anything that dynast or tyrant or dictator has hitherto accomplished. Even the ideal of total equality is a superficial mechanical one, contrary to the nature of things, having no relationship to intrinsic spiritual values, utterly unlike the ideal of democracy. It is indeed dangerous to confuse or identify the two.

Yet some kinds of equality, apart from those directly assured by the structure of democracy, appeal to our sense of what is fair and reasonable, and even where strict equality is ruled out there are extreme inequalities, such as that between abject poverty and grossly superfluous wealth, that appear to us unjustifiable and even intolerable. If then we dismiss, as we must, the equation of democracy and equality, we have still to ask what kinds of equality are congenial to democracy and what kinds of inequality are adverse to it.

This question is too complex and too dependent on changing conditions to receive treatment here. It is enough for our purpose to point to the kind of equality that is most clearly in harmony with the spirit of democracy, that is, equality of opportunity. It is not indeed probable that any form of government can ensure complete equality of opportunity, but democracy, as it progresses, cannot but work in this direction. It can make education free all the way up the line, so that all may develop their gifts for their own advantage and the service of their fellow men. It can remove, to a very great extent, the irrelevant barriers that prevent men from entering the careers for which they are qualified. It can curb the opportunity-reducing controls of wealth and station. It does so by protecting the right to organize. It does so by measures for economic security and by measures for curbing the economic power, and especially the exploitative power, of wealth. In this way, at the same time, it reduces the disparities of wealth as well as of power.

In short, there are two kinds of equality that come squarely within the scope of democracy. One is the equality of civil rights, including the right to count equally with everyone else in the determination of government. This equality is inherent in democracy, in the constitutional frame itself that constitutes a democracy. The other is the equality of opportunity. This equality lies in the ethos, the spirit, of democracy, not in its mere form. Therefore it has to be won by the progressive legislation approved by democratic peoples. It is the fulfilment of the *logic* of the democratic constitution. If the right to equal participation in government, disregarding differences of class and birth and possession and ability, has any sound basis it is that, as the Scottish Robert Burns put it, "a man's a man for a' that." Beyond all those things he has his worth, his dignity, as a man. He has potentialities and aspirations and desires, and they vary endlessly from man to man. Each should have the opportunity of his own. As the leading "Leveller" of the seventeenth century, Rainborough, said: "I think the poorest he that is in England has a life to live as the richest he."

Democracy begins by conferring dignity on the common man and it goes on—and the end of this road is far from being reached—to combine opportunity with dignity. This is as much as can reasonably be asked and it is wiser to proceed along this road than to seek an absolute equality that defeats its own goal— for the latter makes the power of government so overwhelming that it is likely to end in the equality of servitude, which is precisely the opposite of the equality of opportunity.

One of the early critics of democracy, Plato, spoke mockingly of it as a charming system that "assigned equal things to equals and unequals alike." It is within the mission of democracy, and entirely congenial to its nature, that it should remove the insidious inequalities that frustrate and balk the fulfilments men are capable of, the inequalities that arise from cramped circumstances, from the unequal hazards of life, from privilege and from "birth's invidious bar," and from all the tyrannies of man over man, group over group. But there are some inequalities that lie in the very nature of things and there are some inequalities, inequalities irrelevant to the democratic principle, that it cannot afford to disregard. Here is where there is often a misconception about the nature of democracy, and perhaps particularly in the United States, where voters are often called upon to elect officials whose functions involve professional expertness. Democracy cannot afford to disregard the inequalities of capacity and of training for such functions, and it is better that such officials should not be chosen by popular suffrage. This principle applies, for example, to the office of the judge, since the public are unqualified to decide who are best fitted for that office. For positions requiring expert training and professional experience every man is not as good as his neighbor nor is every man equipped to determine who is better than whom. One of the questionable things about Athenian democracy was that it seriously ignored this fact.

At Athens certain offices were filled by resort to the lot. Obviously no important position can be filled that way. It is as ridiculous in public affairs as it would be in private affairs. There is nothing, however, in the democratic principle that calls for the neglect of competence in the determination of office. Democracy gives a supreme role to public opinion, but every well-constructed democracy realizes that the implementation of policy imperatively demands aptitude and experience. Nevertheless there are many still, especially among the more educated and the more privileged, who condemn or find fault with democracy because it "assigns equal things to equals and unequals alike." Such an argument makes two mistakes. It assumes that in a more oligarchical system there is some magic for evoking fitness and for promoting it to power. And it assumes that the selection of the incompetent for administrative or executive functions is inherent in the democratic method. These confusions we shall be dealing with again at a later stage.

In a democracy the public properly decides who its representatives shall be and properly decides between the general policies for which different parties stand. But just as the public cannot properly decide who should be the chief of staff in time of war, for precisely the same reason they should not elect the men who will run the complex administrative and technical affairs of government. It is sometimes loosely said that the "democratic way" to make awards for distinguished services or to determine what is the best novel or play of the year is to appeal to the verdict of "the people"; or that the "democratic way" to run a business or to manage an office is to let the workers direct its affairs. This use of the word "democratic" is ill-considered. Democracy is a *political* system that makes its leaders, its statesmen, its experts, responsible, directly or indirectly, for the way in which they conduct its business. It does not take that business into its own hands or prescribe how it should be done. It could not if it tried, for it would then merely substitute the unqualified and haphazard direction of rough-and-tumble leaders for whatever degree of experience and skill its chosen leaders may possess. The leaders it trusts must choose the experts whom they trust.

The widespread confusion concerning the relation of democracy to equality is an aspect of the deeper confusion concerning democracy and individualism. Democracy gives a new status to the individual, that is, to every person as a person. He is invested with active as well as passive *rights.* He is protected against power and he is endowed with power, the power to share equally with every other citizen in the creation of government. But these rights of the individual do not presume his independence of other men. They do not fence him round within his own little circle. They do not separate his affairs from the affairs of other men, so that he can conduct his affairs without concern for theirs, without regard for the effect on theirs. They do not convey the right to deny the law or to resist the law. They do not validate *laissez-faire.* His rights are other men's obligations, and his obligations are other men's rights. There are no rights in a "state of nature." His rights are social rights and he owns them as a member of society, not as a little sovereign in his own domain. He can claim no rights the exercise of which is demonstrably injurious to his fellow men. He has no right of exploitation. If other men acknowledge his rights it is because they and he are bound together in mutual understanding within a commonwealth. During the period of Jacksonian democracy the sentiment prevailed in most quarters, as it still does in some, that "the best government is that which governs least," and since democracy was "the best government" then democracy meant a system in which there was a minimum of regulation, and especially of economic regulation. In a similar way the term "democracy" is loosely linked with the term "liberty," so that democracy is thought to be attacked whenever any new form of economic regulation or of social legislation is introduced. This viewpoint identifies democracy with the kind of liberalism that grew up in the eighteenth and nineteenth centuries. Conditions are always changing. The relation of man to man and the power of man over man is always changing. No vital principle, such as democracy, can be tied to the body of its own past. The liberties assured by democracy are, as we shall see, more essential, more vital, than any other liberties. So long as we respect and sustain, *directly and indirectly,* these fundamental liberties we remain true to the democratic faith.

Democracy then does not set up "the liberty of the individual" but the liberty of the citizen. His rights as a person are incorporated in his citizenship. His citizenship sustains and affirms his claims as a person, his quality as a human being. Democracy extends rights also to the resident non-citizen, rights as a human being, so that he is safeguarded from the tyrannies of power though he is excluded from participation in the affairs of the state. But all these rights do not sum up to the loose generalization, "the liberty of the individual." This phrase is likely to connote rights in detachment, rights apart from the community, rights apart from obligations, rights unrelated to, or even antagonistic to, the common welfare. We frequently find the irresponsible assertion of such "rights." For example, in his book entitled *The Challenge to Liberty,* ex-President Hoover declared that the various measures included under the New Deal were "a myriad wounds to liberty," and contrary to the principles on which American democracy rests. A considerable majority of Americans had wanted and approved these measures. How far they served the purpose is not our present consideration. Ex-President Hoover challenged them on another ground. His assumption throughout is that economic individualism assures "the liberty of the individual" and that economic regulation destroys that liberty. But he is thinking of the individual as existing in a social vacuum, nor does he raise the question how far one liberty conflicts with other liberties, or how far certain liberties of some may be adverse to certain liberties that others prize, or even to the elementary needs of living. He never seems to realize that liberties of any sort, and not least the liberties guaranteed under democracy, themselves depend on regulation and restraint. There are relative liberties and there are liberties that can be made absolute. Economic liberties must be relative. They must, if wisely devised, be bounded and controlled by consideration of the complex network of economic interdependence that itself exercises utterly variant compulsions on different men and different economic groups. Only the liberties of the mind can be in any sense absolute, for only here is it true that the liberties of some are not intrinsically hampered by the liberties, in the same kind, of others. Within the same community individuals and groups can cherish their respective opinions, their respective faiths, their respective tastes, without thereby making it harder for one another to express their opinions or to cultivate their tastes or to communicate their faiths. But two employers cannot pay different wages or impose on their employees different conditions or different hours of work without making it harder for one of the two to maintain his policy.

Because of the failure to perceive these things, a gross individualism has often paraded itself, especially in the United States, as democratic liberty. This unreflective individualism was associated with the belief in the inevitability of "progress." The optimistic view prevailed that any man can overleap his "birth's invidious bar," that he can overcome the obstacles of poverty—if he wants to, if he cares enough. Because America did, more than any other country, provide examples of men who had risen from rags to riches, because the path had once and again led from log cabin to White House, it was confidently assumed that the life chances of all men depended on themselves. The impediments of adverse conditions were *merely* challenges to the aspiring spirit. Every man, it was assumed, could tap a source of invincible energy to bring him to the goal of his desire. There was a tough, rather brutal, belief in the jostling competition of a world where all men were so like-minded and so like-endowed that the compass of their lives was unerringly set to the true north of pecuniary gain. With it went a simplicity of perception that responded to the continual proclamation of new universal receipts for personal success, such as Yoga and faith-healing and new gadgets for soul-saving and smooth psychological lessons for the cure of mental ills.

It is easy to be supercilious over these folkways—they were after all the defects of the qualities of a period of expansion and no inconsiderable achievement. But the confusion of democratic liberty with the individualistic free-for-all became increasingly detrimental as the times changed. As we shall see more fully in later chapters, it became of imperative importance to the democracy of America that it should attain a more mature understanding of what democracy means.

Chapter Three

———•———

"THE RULE OF THE PEOPLE"

We hear it said that democracy means "the rule of the people." That statement clarifies nothing, for in the strict sense the people never rule. Even in the "direct democracies" of ancient Greece or in the rural cantons of modern Switzerland the people could scarcely be said to be themselves the government. In a modern large-scale state even such approximations to direct popular government as occurred under the conditions just mentioned are unthinkable. You can speak of oligarchy as the rule of the few or of theocracy as the rule of the priests or of monarchy as the rule of the dynast or of dictatorship as the rule of the dictator. These statements, even if they require some qualification, are perfectly understandable and on the whole meaningful. But we cannot equally indicate the nature of democracy by saying it is the rule of the people. Still less admissible is the statement that democracy is "the rule of the masses," for the word "masses" here conveys a suggestion entirely alien to the being of democracy. It suggests the sheer division of a community into two antithetical classes, the elite on the one hand and the undifferentiated multitude on the other. Nor yet do we make the matter sufficiently clear when we say that democracy is the rule of the majority.

Let us look more particularly at this last assertion. Democracy invokes the *majority principle,* not once and for all, but continuously. The majority are not a determinate body who lord it over a minority. In the democratic context the majority must always be rediscovered, must always re-emerge out of the whole. The Greek philosophers thought of democracy as the rule of the poor, of the populace, of *hoi polloi*—in other words, as the rule of a class to which the other classes are subjected. That was before the institutions of the democratic system were developed. To those who have been accustomed to oligarchical systems democracy is likely to mean the antithesis of such systems. In an oligarchy an upper class takes over the domination. Even when the American Constitution was being devised, many of the founders still thought of democracy that way. To John Adams it meant that "the few are at the mercy of the many." To Karl Marx, habituated to German oligarchy, democracy had no other meaning than a reversed class rule with the "proletariat" on top. The modern communist has inherited the misconception. For him the proletariat constitute the people. The communist "vanguard" are the agents of "the people." Therefore, where a Politburo rules with an iron hand there exists a "people's democracy." All such notions are completely out of line with the conclusions to be drawn from the historical development of democracy. Democracy involves the majority principle as a determinant of government, but the only way of invoking this principle assures to every minority certain primary rights—the liberty of opinion with all the other liberties that grow from it. If these liberties are tampered with, democracy ceases to exist. It makes no difference whether it be a majority or a minority that arrogates political liberties exclusively to itself —in either case democracy is dead. Domination by the majority becomes mass domination, which always ends quickly in the rule of the tyrant.

Hence we cannot *define* democracy as majority rule. Under democracy all minorities possess certain major political rights. In a democracy the government, elected by majority vote or more broadly by the process of referring to all the people the election of a government, may take away the privileges or tax down the properties of the minority, but they cannot suppress their opinions or their faiths or their right to appeal to the electorate or their right to due process of law. We cannot claim that a democracy may not do serious hurt to the interests of a minority. But it is profoundly true that it cannot do serious hurt to their consciences or to their convictions or, broadly, to their civil liberties. And so much can be said of no other form of government. Democracy alone offers guarantees against tryanny over the mind and heart of man.

It is a related fallacy that rejects the title of democracy where, though all men have the vote, the influence of some minority is particularly great, because they possess economic power and along with it, not infrequently, control over the most important organs of opinion. The people still freely choose their representatives but they are subject to the influence of the few, subject to indoctrination that induces them to vote for the agents of the "big interests." Where this occurs, we are told it is not democracy at all. And there are those who assert accordingly that democracy is impossible in "capitalist society."

The argument is fallacious. The assumption back of it is that where a few possess much economic power or exercise strong influence over the many, democracy does not, and cannot exist. Let us agree that the concentration of economic power creates great inequality of opportunity, sustains conditions that are prejudicial to democratic ideals, and makes those who are dependent on or subservient to the powerful the instruments of the interests of the few, with little consideration for the welfare of the many. But this admission in no way justifies the conclusion that democracy is at the mercy of economic power. Where the democratic processes are open the people can limit economic power as they see fit, and the degree will depend on their own vigor, their experience, their perception of their own interests. In a democracy those who feel themselves exploited, those who have the same economic interests, can always organize. In the economic struggle numbers are on the side of the economically weaker and through organization numbers can turn weakness into strength. In all democratic countries the citizens, the voters, have put numerous curbs on wealth and on the power of wealth. To claim that a country is not a democracy because there exist great differences in wealth or economic power, while yet political power is at the constitutional disposal of public opinion, is therefore unsound reasoning. The extreme form of this fallacious reasoning is the assertion constantly made by the upholders of Soviet communism, to the effect that other countries are sham democracies, whereas in the Soviet Union true democracy reigns—in a country where the people have no voice whatever in major public concerns and where unmitigated irresponsible power holds everyone in its relentless grip.

But, it is objected, how can you speak of democracy where a few rich men own the great newspapers and the other agencies of communication, where they control the movies, where they hold the positions of greatest prestige, where they set up vigilant lobbies to promote their own interests, where they have in their hands every means to persuade, to cajole, to bribe, to propagandize? It is an implicit testimonial to democracy that we have a temptation to deny the name to those democracies that harbor features of which we disapprove. But there is error here also. It is one thing to adjudge whether a country is a democracy, it is another to assess how well or how effectively it employs its democratic facilities. No state, democratic or other, can rise higher than the standards set by its own people. Democracies, like all other states, vary greatly in energy and in quality.

But apart from this broad consideration we should observe that in a democracy all groups, all interests, have the right to appeal and to propagandize. The means at the disposal of various groups may be very unequal, but we have already pointed out that the final control of economic resources remains always at the discretion of the electorate. That is why we should not speak as though there were two kinds of democracy, economic democracy and political democracy. Again, under the democratic system the people often give ear to the appeal of groups and parties that have against them the majority of the great newspapers and of the other organs of communication. In Europe, since 1870, minority parties possessing at the start very small resources have grown to

majority parties, even where, as in Germany, nearly all the
agencies of influence and of prestige were on the other side. In
the United States and in England the people have put into office
on several occasions the party that had the weight of newspaper
opinion against it. Parties have sometimes won out where they had
a quite negligible press, as when in Ontario a farmers' group under Drury defeated the old-established parties, though it had not a
single influential newspaper supporting it. In short, democracy
permits the tides of opinion to flow and to change direction.
Democracy in action ensures that all opinions obtain the opportunity to be heard and it can at need correct the balance if some of
these opinions are backed by greater economic resources than are
others.

Obviously, if many people are indoctrinated in some set of
opinions these opinions are heard more persistently and more
often than if they were held only by a few. Democracy is always
seething with the movements and changes of opinion. In this
flux minority opinions have their chance. New leaders arise and
win a following. New movements grow and old ones fade. Always the many are influenced by the few. But to claim that this
condition is undemocratic is to be totally unrealistic. Those who
make this claim do not really object to the fact of leadership. They
want instead their own prophets and their own spell-binders to be
in the saddle. Then we shall have "true democracy." In their eyes,
a democracy is the kind of government that supports their policies.

Whoever leads, whoever influences the people, it is democracy,
so long as the avenue to government is free election by the majority. Democracy does not make people wise and good, it does not
assure that they shall vote according to their true needs or best
interests. It merely gives them the opportunity. Under democracy
there will always be minority voices, there will always be minority
organs of opinion. There will always be both incentive and freedom for minority leaders to make their appeal. There will always
be some dissatisfaction with the government in power. The people
will always have the opportunity to respond to new appeals. The
processes of re-education are always available under democracy.

We see now why the simple analogy that makes democracy mean "the rule of the people," as monarchy means the rule of the king or dictatorship the rule of the dictator, is very misleading. The function of the people is not to govern but to make the government constitutionally responsible to, and utterly dependent on, its will. And the only way the people with their multitudinous differences can have a will at all is through the uncontrolled right of the whole citizen body to register in a concerted operation their choice between contestants for the right to govern. On occasion they may register also their approval or disapproval of specific measures submitted for their consideration, but their main function is to choose their political representatives. This kind of choosing is rendered workable through the party system, which roughly organizes major differences of opinion—or of interest—around opposing programs of action.

All this may seem obvious enough, and yet there are those who condemn democracy because, they say, the people are unfit to rule. And there are those who, in a more friendly spirit, deplore the plight of democracy because the people simply cannot undertake the task it imposes on them, the task of coping with all the complex issues of modern government. In one of his earlier books, *The Phantom Public*, Walter Lippmann put forward the plaint that the democratic man was baffled and disenchanted. He could not make his sovereign voice heard concerning a thousand tangled affairs, and how could he? How could he have an effective opinion about the situation in China today and about the sewers of Brooklyn tomorrow, and the next day about the effects of subsidies to agriculture, and the next day about some deal with Yugoslavia, and so on without end? He gave it up. He was disillusioned about democracy. He could not live up to its demands.

If any "man in the street" holds these views about his democratic obligations it is quite proper he should be disillusionized. But not, we hope, about democracy. Only about his illusions about democracy. Representative democracy, the only kind that has any meaning under modern conditions, does not put any such impossible strain on the citizen. The people, let us repeat, do not and cannot govern; they control the government. In every live democracy they decide the broad march of politics. They decide whether there is to be more social legislation or less, more collectivization or somewhat more play for private enterprise, more dependence on an international system of security or more self-sufficiency and relative isolation, and so forth. They decide these issues, not one at a time but by voting for an administration favorable to one or another "platform." They decide them partly—and in the last resort—at the polls, and partly by the continuously manifested indications of public sentiment. To make decisions easier there is in every community a sense of alternative directions, marked respectively left and right, and a sway of opinion in one or the other direction. The signposts marking "left" and "right" may not always be clear, but they are always understood. The greater trends in either direction reveal the deep hidden workings of group and folk consciousness, down on a level that the recorders of opinion-changes and the political forecasters never fathom and sometimes entirely ignore.

This incessant activity of popular opinion is the dynamic of democracy. It decides between the larger alternatives of policy-making and in that way has an impact on a thousand issues. Mr. Lippmann, in the book referred to, was clearly off the beam when he suggested that it is not the business of the public to decide the substantive policies of government but merely to see that the government abides by the rules, like a referee who watches the players but takes no part in the game. The greater changes in the socio-economic policies of Western European countries in the nineteenth and twentieth centuries—the whole trend towards social legislation and the control of economic power—were due to the swelling currents of public opinion, responsive to changing conditions. Or we may cite the more recent experience of the United States, where a new manifestation of public opinion, opposed by most of the prestige-bearers and of the well-to-do, carried to power and maintained in power the party of the "New Deal."

That is how the citizens of a democracy make their citizenship effective. Not as individuals deciding for themselves the successive problems of politics, each in speculative detachment registering his opinion on every issue. Not merely as units casting their separate votes every few years as election time comes round—the citizens of a democracy are *continuously* engaged in a massive give-and-take of creative opinion-making. Certainly not as experts who must willy-nilly do the job of the administration, that is, by finding the answers to the very specific questions that the administration must face from day to day. No business is run that way, and no government can be. Executive jobs are for executives, whether in business or in government. The public—or the workers or the shareholders—may very well entertain an opinion on whether the management is doing well or badly, but that is a different matter altogether.

We observe in passing that in a democracy there are two stages of decision-making before the *proper* job of the expert begins. First, there is the primary function of policy-making, the choice between directions, the function of the people. Second, there is the delineation of policy by the legislators and the heads of the government—in accordance with the "mandate" thus entrusted to them. Third, there is the implementation of policy. At this third stage the expert finds his place. It is here, and here alone, that he belongs. He is the technician or the craftsman in the art of government.

It is an eminently logical system. The representatives of the people have the authority. They are presumably—they always become at least—more conversant with the ways of governing than are the lay citizens, but they are not experts. They mark out the lines of advance and the experts build the roads. The logic is admirable, but as in all human affairs it is subject to distortion. These three functions are not clear-cut and separable in practice. The limits of each in relation to the others must be discretionary and flexible. Which means also that there may be conflict, confusion, and encroachment between the participants. The legislator may not let the expert do his proper job or, more commonly, he permits the expert to follow his own devices into the area of policy-making. The cabinet officers may ignore the spirit of their mandate, particularly in the screened-off sector of foreign policy. The expert may become a worshipper of routine, a jealous guardian of the secrets of office, a bureaucrat in the less honorable sense of the word.

Such things happen everywhere, and perhaps there is no safeguard except the vigilance of the public, as it becomes better educated in the ways of democracy and armed with fuller knowledge of its practical operation. What indeed appears throughout, as we study democracy at work, is that the defects and shortcomings it exhibits are due not to any inherent weakness in its principle but to the greater responsibilities it imposes on those who carry it out. These responsibilities are in themselves reasonable and never excessive, but interest and pride and office are always at hand, to deflect, to distort, and to betray. The ever-active democratic process checks these tendencies. How effectively it does so is in the keeping of the public, who have the authority and the means to control those whom they entrust with the business of governing.

Chapter Four

———•—•———

ANOTHER KIND OF DEMOCRACY?

A new and particularly beguiling misconception has gained hold in recent times. It has misled a number of people who have democratic sympathies and it has been assiduously propagated by others who have no use whatever for democracy. It depends on a distinction they draw between two kinds of democracy, called respectively "political" and "economic" democracy. We hear them say that the democracy we have is not real because we don't have democracy in the plant and in the office, in the bank and in the industrial corporation. The charge is made that in the United States and other "democratic" countries we have *only* political democracy, whereas what matters far more is economic democracy. They say that if they had to make a choice between the two they would always choose economic democracy. The more unrealistic among them declare that if Soviet Russia lacks the political kind at least that country is blessed by its enjoyment of the economic kind. Henry Wallace was leaning in the same direction when he said: "Some in the United States believe that we have over-emphasized what might be called political or Bill of Rights democracy." In the same spirit Harold Laski has maintained that ours is a "capitalist democracy" and that capitalist democracy suffers from an incurable disease, "for the simple reason" that it "has lost the power to win assent to its hypotheses." "It is against the conditions inherent in capitalism that men revolt."

Whatever may be the merits of the changes advocated by those who use this language there is an intellectual confusion in the language they use. Democracy means literally the rule of the people. The way democracy implements this rule, the only way in a complex society, is by assigning to the people the right to make and to change the government through a majority or plurality of their votes. The way this right is exercised, the only way, is by the free expression and free organization of opinion, so that if the majority disapprove the "hypotheses" of any established system they can and will change the system. Under democracy, operating in this way, if the people refuse assent to any policies of government these policies no longer prevail.

In this country, if or when the people want to dethrone the capitalistic system, they have the power to do it. They don't need to "revolt" against it—they can vote against it. If they don't vote against it it is because a majority still "assent to its hypotheses." Actually, given democratic conditions, the people never vote into existence or out of existence a whole established system. They never feel the need to do so, because public opinion is constantly active and creates a kind of moving equilibrium between institutions and desires. That is why, incidentally, no democratic system today sustains a purely capitalist economy. What we have in democratic countries is an amalgam of capitalistic and collectivist elements, an economic order better called socio-capitalism than merely capitalism. It is the way of revolutionaries to think only of drastic opposites, to construe political action as always the fateful decision between the two. This way of thinking is contrary to the habituations of democracy. A democratic public senses the need of change. If it is vigilant it will sense the need for a series of changes that cumulatively, over the longer stretch, will mean transformations far more thoroughgoing and far more deeply rooted than the all-or-nothing methods of the revolutionary ever achieve. The revolutionary thinks only of the moment; the democrat has longer thoughts.

These changes are economic and social changes. In a democracy the economic system, however good or however bad it is, is that which is in rough accord with prevailing opinion. It is perfectly true that the opinion of the public may be much influenced by those whose interest it is to maintain a particular system. What then? They have also the opportunity to hear the contrary arguments of Mr. Laski. He gets a most impressive audience. They have also the opportunity to hear Mr. Marcantonio and Mr. Wallace and Mr. Norman Thomas and Mr. Dewey and Mr. Truman—and, for that matter, Mr. Stalin. The people may be misled; even the wisest may be misled. Where is supreme wisdom to be found? What leader of the people has no axe to grind? What group does not preach its own gospel with more concern for success than for the nice discrimination of the truth? So be it. We are all human, and humans are all subject to deception. They seek to persuade one another, and even when they do it in the sheer conviction that they are preaching the truth they may still be grossly mistaken. What then is the way out? What kind of utopia is pure of propagandism? Where on earth does the clear light of heaven shine without some atmosphere that intercepts its rays? In this world of uncertainties and half lights the only hope of the people is that they have access to all opinions, can choose as best they are qualified to choose, and can change their minds if they find out that they have erred. This is what democracy offers. And although there are many imperfections in the offering it remains the only way of political salvation.

Let us keep the record clear. There is no other kind of democracy. If the people have the rights and the liberties that enable them in a constitutional way to make and to unmake government, there and there alone democracy exists. Where it exists, it is not some qualified form to be called capitalist democracy or socialist democracy. There are not two opposing kinds of democracy respectively named "political" and "economic." Indeed, it is exceedingly hard to give any genuine meaning to the expression, "economic democracy." We know what "economic security" means or "economic opportunity" or even "economic equality." But it is a misuse of language to call any of these things, in so far as they exist, "economic democracy." We know what socialism means and what capitalism means, but there is no necessary relation between the presence of socialism and the presence of democracy or between the presence of capitalism and the absence of democracy.

Sometimes we find the expression "social democracy" used in place of "economic democracy," with the same antithesis to "political democracy." We are told that social democracy is a much more inclusive system, or that it is the goal to which political democracy is the means, or that it is the substance or essence of democracy whereas political democracy is merely the form. Now there is no reason why those who believe in democracy should not seek to lessen the disparities of wealth and to socialize one part after another of the economy. So long as they accept the democratic process they will move by degrees, not by a sudden overturn of the pre-established order. They will advance experimentally, taking advantage of favorable public opinion and not attempting to overstep the bounds of majority acceptance. Proceeding thus, they will learn to what extent a socialistic economy is compatible, under the given conditions, with the maintenance of democracy. For socialism emphatically does not *mean* democracy, and there is always the question how far the concentrated and monopolized power of a socialistic system can coexist with the effective responsibility of government to the suffrage of the people. On this subject there has been a division of opinion ever since the principle of socialism appeared on the horizon of modern politics. Thus the author of *Democracy in America,* Alexis de Tocqueville, roundly declared that "democracy and socialism—are not only different, they are opposed." No one can honestly deny that they are different; it is still an open question whether they are necessarily opposed, though the examples we have of *totally* socialized economies do nothing to lessen the doubt.

When, however, those who live under a system where socialism in some sense exists, but where the democratic liberty of opinion is wholly absent, assert with unblushing vehemence that they alone enjoy democracy or "true" democracy we reach an area where the assertion of identity is sacerdotal and final. Socialism *is* democracy, capitalism *is* slavery, and that is the end of it. Dictatorship over the proletariat is dictatorship *of* the proletariat. The proletariat *are* the people. The democracy of "the toilers" is complete because "the exploiters" have been liquidated. The government is the agent of the interests of the toilers, their real interests. It matters not that no "toiler" dare vote against the Party; nor that he cannot change his toil without a permit; nor that he cannot move from place to place without the sanction of the powers above. He still enjoys true freedom—so he is told by those who tightly hold the reins of power. Should he ever doubt it he must cherish his heresy in secret. It is dangerous to talk.

We shall have later occasion to consider some other aspects of this remarkable power-myth that uses the mysterious words "true democracy" with the same unction that characterized the equal and opposite totalitarianism of Adolf Hitler. It is enough at this point to reiterate the simple and obvious truth that democracy and socialism have different references, that democracy is a way of governing and being governed and that socialism is a kind of social economy. *How* the two are and may be related is a question the answer to which, after all our argumentation, will come from the history of the world now in the making.

Before we leave the subject we may find it helpful to consider the relation between democracy, as a way of organizing the great state, and analogous institutional procedures within more limited associations. We speak, for example, of "trade union democracy" or "church democracy" or "college democracy," and so forth. What we mean is that the members of the organization in question conduct or participate in its affairs or that they vote on its policies. Obviously this is not a matter to be determined by the state, but only by the members themselves. Men belong to these various organizations not as citizens, not as members of the state, but as particular groups sharing particular interests that distinguish them from other groups sharing other interests. Since there is no specific word for, say, the exercise of control by the members of a trade union over the affairs of their union or the exercise of control by shareholders over the affairs of their corporation we borrow the word "democracy." The meaning is clear enough and the usage creates no problem except when people assume that democracy in its proper sense requires or implies that trade unions and corporations and colleges and churches existing under that democracy must be governed in the same way.

The assumption has no validity. Voluntary organizations, like the church or the trade union, are free under democracy to organize their affairs in their own way, except so far as they use their power to the public hurt. If, for example, an employers' organization misrepresents its products or exacts extortionate prices or curtails the supply of a commodity or establishes a monopoly it is or may properly be subject to governmental action. Or if a trade union or a professional organization practises discrimination against any group of citizens or flagrantly disregards the public welfare it is or may properly be controlled by government. But its internal organization, apart from such manifest consequences to the commonwealth, is its own concern. A "self-governing" private organization is one thing; a "self-governing" state is quite another.

There are considerations that may make this type of "self-government" difficult, unwieldy, or undesirable in the case of certain voluntary organizations. Much depends on the nature of the interests for which they stand. These interests may not be such that they are most successfully pursued under a system that puts the direction of affairs in the suffrage of the members. The pursuit of the organization's interests may demand a specialized expertness that is manifested by accomplishment in terms of standards recognized by the membership, so that they willingly leave the direction to those who have proved their capacity. Many kinds of association, from a missionary society to a political party, may fall into this category. The membership again may be indefinite or it may fall into various grades of members who possess very different qualifications. It is doubtful whether any great business can be conducted "democratically," even though it is always desirable that one way or another those engaged in the business should have confidence in the executive and should feel that they are integrally bound to its decisions. This condition can sometimes be assured through one or another form of consultation. Again, it is often difficult, in the case of various specialized organizations, to say who are really "members" of them and in what sense. Are the alumni "members" of a college and, if they are in some sense, should they on that account vote its educational policies? Do the shareholders constitute the membership of a business corporation? They have one right that suggests it, the right to vote for the directors of the organization and thus in a sense to control its affairs. But they usually know far less about these affairs than do the management or the office staff or the working force. They usually have little interest in the concern beyond the receipt of as big dividends as may be, and very few of them ever turn up at the annual meeting. Not out of such stuff is democracy made. Who, again, are the "members" of a hospital? Shall we include the nurses, the orderlies, the patients—or only the doctors? Frequently such organizations have a special category of presumably qualified persons, who alone select the leadership, like the cardinals of the papal order.

Finally, there is one conclusive difference between all these organizations and the great state. The state alone has direct coercive power over men, including the members of all other organizations. The way that sovereign power is applied is of vital concern to all men. Nor is there any security against unbridled tyranny and oppression unless this power is made responsible to the whole people. Other organizations have limited interests and whatever rights and privileges they enjoy are limited by the regulatory function of government. Democracy is the *political* system that harnesses over-ruling power to the will of the people. In this fundamental respect there is no analogy between democracy in its proper sense and the self-government of other associations.

In his discerning little book, *The Essentials of Democracy*, A. D. Lindsay draws a contrast between the comfortable democracy of the old-time town-meeting or of the local brotherhood and the more difficult and much less intimate representative democracy that is all we can attain in a modern state. He holds that "the inspiration of modern democracy came from the entirely satisfactory character of democratic government in the Christian congregation," particularly from such seventeenth century Protestant groups as the Independents, the Anabaptists, and the Quakers. We agree that "the decisions of the small society, when it is working happily, are felt to be the decisions of every member." But this kind of unanimity is possible only where the strong particular tie of a common cause unites the group—and even then it is a tender plant, most liable to be blown down by the blasts of dissension. Democracy must be tough enough not only to admit differences but to *use* them. The congregation of the like-minded is an entirely different configuration from the community that must include all manner of men and still create a workable government —a government that is invested with coercive power. Nor can we accept the claim that the local congregation was the inspiration of modern democracy. The roots of democracy in England went back much further than the seventeenth century. It arose from a long series of successful attempts to resist the exactions and oppressions of irresponsible government, through movements that gradually extended from the higher to the lower social classes. The oppressive hierarchy of the established church was linked with the obduracy of the crown. In the seventeenth century the English middle classes developed a remarkable spirit of resistance to both, asserting at the same time the right of parliament against the king and the right of the individual conscience against the bishops.

In passing we observe that the historical role of religion in the development of democracy has been indirect rather than direct. It did not do much to promote democracy by precept and example —for the most part it was undemocratic in spirit—but it was of profound importance in stimulating resistance to the claims of the secular power over doctrinal or ecclesiastical affairs. It could appeal to a higher authority. Thus armed, it broke down the totalitarian pretensions of government, and prepared the way for attacks on other than religious grounds. As soon as the one church indivisible of the Middle Ages was rifted by schisms and the rise of protestant faiths the absolute state fought a losing war to maintain the unity of government and religious authority. Each religious brotherhood tenaciously insisted on its own liberty, though frequently, when it came to power, it proved as authoritarian as the state itself. This authoritarianism was particularly characteristic of Calvinism and certain forms of Puritanism.

This issue, however, is not our present concern. We are concerned merely to show that over the whole realm of government there is only one way of governing that has any title to be called democracy, that there is no *alternative* way to be distinguished as economic democracy, and that where democracy exists it leaves certain very important organizations, such as the church, free to set up within themselves their own forms of discipline, as seems best to their respective members, so long as they do not encroach on the liberties that democracy assures to all men within its bounds.

Chapter Five

———•—•———

THE ARISTOCRATIC FALLACY

It is one thing to identify democracy, another to comprehend it, to realize its nature and import. It has been and still is grievously misunderstood, and never was it more essential than today that those who are fortunate enough to live under democratic rule should think about it in clear terms. Many of the indictments of democracy made by those who enjoy its fundamental liberties, even by prominent philosophers, witness to a lack of comprehension. Let us consider from this point of view one of the oldest and most persistent of misunderstandings. It was the ground on which democracy was rejected by Plato and given a mixed reception by Aristotle—though in fairness to these great thinkers it should be remembered that when they wrote they had before them only one turbulent manifestation of democracy, grossly limited as it was by a slave-bound economy and running its brief and precarious course in an age when the social and educational conditions of enduring democracy had not yet been attained. No such excuse can be put forward on behalf of the modern philosophers who take a similar position.

Of the ancient philosophers Plato was particularly hostile to democracy. Politics should be the charge of those who know, the experts, the enlightened, the "guardians," as he called them in the *Republic*. It is not for the unruly populace, the creatures of appetite. When they get control they make an unholy mess of things. There is one right way of ruling, and the uneducated masses are ignorant of it, regardless of it. They create nothing but disorder, and the end of it all is tyranny. The wild beast takes over.

Men of high ethical principles, as Plato was, may be more dangerous as political advisers, and more likely to do grievous evil if they come to power, than men of lesser breed. Plato was above all the moral aristocrat who, given the opportunity, would have translated his precepts into laws binding on all men. He made no reckoning of human nature nor of the danger of coercive morality nor of the greeds and corruptions of power nor of the ordinary needs of ordinary men. Least of all did he perceive that the very tyranny he feared was the inevitable outcome of the disdain he felt for the masses, and of the uncontrolled authority he claimed for his elite—even if by some miracle any ruling elite could have been endowed with the ascetic virtue that he preached.

Similar misapprehensions have been cultivated by moderns who have behind them vastly more recorded history from which to learn better. Whenever men separate themselves from the bulk of their fellow men, especially when they think that their higher culture entitles them to think meanly of the average citizen, they are apt to nourish the aristocratic fallacy. The fallacy lies not in their claim to be "aristocrats"—that claim may or may not be justified—but in the doctrine they on that account entertain concerning the nature of government and especially concerning the significance of democracy.

Democracy, they say, is the rule of the incompetent. It puts the average man on the throne. The average man is opaque to new ideas, blind to new needs, obfuscated, routinized, uncomprehending—in short, unfit to rule. All quality, all achievement, all advance, comes from the few, the elite. Apart from them mankind would still be living in the mud huts of the primaeval savage. When the elite are bereft of power and the masses, contrary to the first law of existence, are exalted over them, everything is reduced "to a dead level of incapacity."

Democracy is not the rule of "the masses" nor is it something for "the masses" only. Democracy is not the enthronement of mediocrity, to the disadvantage of the elite, the enlightened, the cultivated. Democracy is the political liberation of *all* men from the chains of power. Democracy in origin and in action is a system devised to break the primal source of all tyranny, which is the coercive power of group over group, or of the few over the many. It is not the "common man" alone who has suffered from the irresponsibility of power, from "the oppressor's wrong, the proud man's contumely," from "the insolence of office, and the spurns that patient merit of the unworthy takes," from the worst insolence of all, which says in effect: "I have power over you, therefore what I believe about man and God, about science and art, about life and society, about right and wrong, you *must* believe." Those who suffer most from this oppression, who find it most intolerable, are the true elite among men, the thinkers, the artists, the men of deep faith, the men of generous heart and of free spirit, the creators of all that has enriched and ennobled mankind, those who search beneath the appearance of things, those who wrestle with the unknown, those who dream and those who aspire. Unmitigated power has most of the time sought to crush and tame them, to enslave them, and when it has failed it has consigned them to the dungeon, the scaffold, the stake, and the cross. And often enough the indoctrinated masses have cried out, "Crucify him," taking sides with power.

Democracy provides the way of liberation alike from mass intolerance and from the ruthlessness and corruption of power. Democracy, when it has time enough to operate, dissolves the very concept of "the masses." If by "the masses" we mean an undifferentiated aggregate of people, sharing a common lot—usually one of ignorance and poverty—behaving in a de-individualized crowd-like manner, unthinking, indiscriminate, rudely responsive to the hot appeals and cheap slogans of the loud-voiced orator, then "the masses" are a phenomenon characteristic of undemocratic class-bound societies and utterly uncongenial to the genius of democracy. *The expression itself has much vogue only in the less democratic countries.* It or its equivalent was in regular use in Germany,

Russia, and other oligarchical regimes. Thence it was taken over by the Marxists, since it is in harmony with the thinking of those who regard the state—all states but their own—as the mere organization of class against class, the exploiting class against "the masses." Democracy in operation brings into being a new order, no longer class-bound, and as "the masses" learn its ways and gain its rights and opportunities they cease to be masses any more. In the days of the Founding Fathers the thinking of this country was still, in the main, oligarchical. In those days prominent statesmen could still speak, with the usual connotation of contempt, of "the masses," the "inferior sort," the "lower orders." As American democracy gained hold and became conscious of itself that mode of speech became obsolete. "The masses" were transformed into the people. When we say "the people" we draw no line between class and class. If we speak of "the sovereignty of the people" we are no longer thinking of a lower breed, but of all men together in their capacity as citizens. When we say "the people," we speak with respect and not with derogation. Democracy draws no line between the noble and the vulgar, as two classes of men, one of which holds political prerogative, one of which is debased as well as powerless. Democracy gives equal rights to all men. And in doing so it breaks all barriers of education, of culture, and of opportunity, that formerly set men hopelessly apart, as preordained inferiors and superiors.

It is to be deplored that certain men of letters, philosophers, artists, and other sophisticated persons still look down on democracy from ivory towers and sum it up as the rule of mediocrity, as the "cult of incompetence," as the "vulgarization of society," as the reduction of political life to the lowest common denominator, and so forth. Whoever propounds or suggests this thesis, whether he be a sheltered philosopher like Santayana or a professor of poetry like Faguet or an amateur Darwinian like Madison Grant or a professor of government like Sait, cannot have read history very deeply or very understandingly. Aloof criticism of this type, without consideration of the realistic alternatives to democracy, lacks a sense of proportion. Critics of this type usually live under democratic conditions where they are constitutionally protected from the grosser abuses of power. They do not realize that the "aristocracy" they yearn for is an idle dream. They do not comprehend the imperatives of the political struggle or the fierce hunger for naked power that is loosed wherever the restraints of democracy do not hold. And they do not seem to comprehend that the cultural liberty they enjoy is itself a right that democracy alone ensures.

There are enough vulgarians and enough incompetents in every society. They are to be found on every level. Ancient lineage or noble birth is no guarantee against incompetence nor even against vulgarity. There has been much vulgarity, thinly disguised by a veneer of manners, in royal courts. The incompetence of kings has been a tragic commonplace of history. There is no ground for thinking that democracy breeds vulgarity or encourages incompetence. On the contrary, the equality of rights that democracy bestows is calculated to raise, not to lower, the standards of the ordinary man. Men are apt to behave according to the social expectations of this behavior. If they are treated as inferiors, if they cannot rise or show their worth, if they are denied the opportunities of higher endeavor, if they cannot emerge from the mean cares of a mean environment, then their habits and their thought may conform to their circumstances. There was shrewd truth in the saying of Bernard Shaw that the difference between a flower-girl and a duchess is not how she behaves but how she is treated. And it is noteworthy that the English poet who more than any man of his time attacked vulgarity and "philistinism"—Matthew Arnold—found that one strongly predisposing condition was the social stigma of inferiority. "Can it be denied," he said, "that to live in a society of equals tends in general to make a man's spirits expand and his faculties work easily and actively; while to live in a society of superiors, although it may occasionally be very good discipline, yet in general tends to tame the spirits and to make the play of the faculties less secure and active? Can it be denied that to be heavily overshadowed, to be

profoundly insignificant, has, on the whole, a depressing and be-
numbing effect on the character?"

There is yet another consideration that is ignored by those who
look down on democracy as the rule of incompetence. Their argument runs somewhat as follows. The people are incompetent to
rule, therefore to govern them they will choose those who are as
incompetent as themselves. The incompetent don't want competence, or they do not recognize it when they see it. This simple
reasoning is not true for ordinary affairs. Most of us know little
or nothing about, say, plumbing or law, but we want to choose a
good plumber or a good lawyer when we need him, and we are
perfectly ready to take advice on the subject. There is, of course, a
difference between choosing a lawyer or a physician and choosing
a representative. We must not press the analogy. Our particular
interests and our emotions are more likely in the latter case to
divert our attention from questions of competence. Obviously a
democracy will not function well unless the people have some
degree of social education. But democracy alone permits and indeed
stimulates this social education.

Historical exhibits of democracy, in Britain and the British
Dominions, in Scandinavia, in Western Europe, in the United
States itself, do not justify the charge of incompetence, least of all
when we compare the processes of democracy with those of other
systems. Competence in governing is not indeed the mark of any
form of government; wisdom in governing is again all too rare a
phenomenon. Under any system there are weak governments and
strong ones, better governments and worse ones. The charge of
vulgarization is not put to any test of comparative evidence. In a
democracy "the vulgar" do not form a party, opposed by a losing
party of the "non-vulgar." Policies are not made that way nor
legislators elected. Sometimes in a democracy a boss or dema-
gogue, an uncultured tough spoilsman who sells cheap favors for
votes, gains control and makes government his private racket.
This phenomenon has its best illustrations in the United States.
It has occurred mostly, however, in local government, in the great

cities where large immigrant populations, untrained in the ways of democracy, still feeling themselves aloof from all relation to public policy, living in relative poverty in huddled colonies, were an easy prey for the smooth "ward-heeler." Where the people are politically ignorant the boss has his opportunity. But where the people are ignorant democracy has not done its work.

The charge of incompetence, levelled against the *principle* of democracy, is equally unjustified. The leadership of democracy, in times of grave crisis, compares favorably enough with the leadership of states that put no trust in the people. Democracy has the opportunity to change its supreme leaders and often, in times of crisis, has exercised its right to do so by promoting to power the man of destiny. The two World Wars bore salient witness to this capacity. It is particularly significant that Britain chose for its war-time ruler a statesman whom it had rejected in times of peace and whom it removed from power when he had triumphantly carried the people through to victory. They recognized his magnificent capacity to lead them in war—and in war alone. Could any non-democratic state have displayed such discernment? Let us remember also that it is in non-democratic states that leaders put their trust in sheer aggressive power, and aggressive power often makes fatal miscalculations. Roosevelt and Churchill would never have led their peoples to ruinous disaster, as did Hitler and Mussolini.

There is another and more subtle way in which the aristocrat, especially the moral aristocrat, misapprehends the service of democracy. The aristocrat is a poor psychologist. His aloofness, his sense of superiority, prevents him from sensing what would be the reactions of the people to the rules he would impose on them. Thus he misjudges the conditions on which their well-being depends. He wants "good government" but the only good government is one the rules of which are made by him or by his kind. Like Plato, he knows where everybody belongs in the scheme of things—and that is where they *ought* to belong, according to his standards. He himself would be happy and would feel free under the system of authority he approves. So he fancies that everybody ought to be happy and feel free under that system, and he easily slips—poor psychologist that he is—into the persuasion that because they *ought* to be they *would* be.

This misapprehension is revealed in many ways, but we shall be content briefly to refer to one of them. It consists in the identification of liberty with acceptance of the moral or cultural code of the aristocrat. If they are free in obeying the law they approve then everybody is free who obeys it, even against his desire or his will. Liberty, says Father Sheen, is not the right to do as you please but "the right to do whatever you *ought*." True liberty, said Irving Babbitt, "is not liberty to do what one likes but liberty to adjust oneself to law." These are modern echoes of an old perversion of meaning, dear to authoritarians of every school. Liberty, they say, is "obedience to law," to the true law, *their* law, the law of *their* dogma, the law of *their* God. Let them hold to their dogmas, let them worship their Gods, but they do it with cleaner hands and with purer hearts if they refrain from the ironic falsehood that when they force others to do the same, that is, for others, liberty.

How well such statements chime with the words of Hitler or the words of, say, the Nazi apologist Othmar Spann, that "liberty, in positive terms, is not doing what I please but doing—what I ought to do." Whenever men seek to condone the killing of liberty they point in another direction and say, "look, liberty is not dead; that was only its false appearance. Here is true liberty." And to support their sophistications they can go back to the metaphysical obscurities of the absolutist philosopher Hegel or to the ominous words of the ambiguous prophet Rousseau, when he said that men could be "forced to be free."

———◆———

Chapter Six

A WAY OF GOVERNING AND

BEING GOVERNED

We have been stressing the point that democracy must be understood in the first instance as a *political* system. From the beginning of its usage the word has denoted a form of government in its relation to a people. Animating that form there is what we may call the spirit of democracy. But we must beware of *defining* democracy as a "spirit," a creed, a way of living, a set of attitudes. If we do so we play into the hands of those who claim that their systems of government express "true" democracy or "real" democracy or a "higher" democracy, even when these systems carry authoritarianism to the limit and mock all the rights historical democracy has won. It is true on the other hand that the empty form of democracy can be paraded before a people, as has been done so many times in Latin-American countries and as was done in Soviet Russia when the new constitution was announced by Stalin in 1936. But when we say that democracy must be defined as a political form or system we obviously mean that if any system is to be named democratic it must be genuinely organized in correspondence with the designated form. Democracy is a particular kind of political system. Democracy exists where that system *operates,* not where misleading orators or hollow proclamations assert that it exists.

Democracy, then, is not a creed, though it involves a creed. It is not a "spirit" or a way of living, though it endures only where men's hearts and habits are attuned to its demands. It is not a doctrine of human nature, though it invests the human being, as man and as citizen, with rights that imply the value and the integrity of his personality. It is not any particular brand of opinion, concerning the economic order of a society or any such matters, for it leaves all kinds of opinion free and it can function only through the free organization of opinion differences. It is instead a way of governing and of being governed, maintaining through relevant institutions a certain structure of civil and political rights or liberties.

What then is this way of governing? We indicate it—but we do not yet identify it—when we say that democracy constitutionally guarantees certain fundamental rights to all citizens. Apart from these rights—the right to think and believe after one's own mind and heart, the right to express one's opinions and to organize for their furtherance, the right to vote according to one's opinions, and so forth—democracy cannot exist. But the rights in question are not the same thing as a form of government. They may properly be made a *test* of its existence but they do not constitute it. Secretary of State George C. Marshall applied this test when the Western Powers were in dispute with Soviet Russia regarding the implementation of a pledge made under the Yalta agreement of 1945. The allied plenipotentiaries pledged themselves to use "democratic means" for the solution of the problems of the occupied countries of Europe, and again at the Berlin Conference they gave directions "for the eventual reconstruction of German political life on a democratic basis." But when it came to performance the Soviet Union and the Western powers were completely opposed, the former claiming that its own restrictive and high-handed methods were in accordance with the democratic pledge. General Marshall insisted that the essence of democracy was the recognition that "human beings have certain inalienable rights—that is, rights that may not be given or taken away," and that until these rights were granted and guaranteed the pledge was not fulfilled. These rights included "the right of every individual to develop his mind and his soul in the ways of his own choice, free of fear and coercion—provided only that he does not interfere with the rights of others." "To us," he said, "a society is not free if law-abiding citizens live in fear of being denied the right to work or being deprived of life, liberty and the pursuit of happiness."

The argument was just, in the light of the whole history of what the world has known as democracy. For our purpose of definition, however, we must look beyond the possession of such rights to the constitutional order that gives and guards the assurance. This constitutional order, in any of its varieties, *is* democracy. Now then we must ask: what kind of order is it that can *constitutionally* assure these rights? We find that both historically and logically it is an order that, to establish the right of opinion, gives free opinion itself a politically creative role. In other words, the government must be dependent on, and responsive to, the changes of public opinion. More closely, each successive administration is voted into office by an election or series of elections at which the people freely express their effective preference for one group of candidates over another group or other groups. In order that this process may be constitutionally possible the law must bind the relations of men in the areas to which it applies but must not bind their opinions in any areas. (We shall not pause here to examine the apparent but not genuine exceptions to this principle that fall under laws relating to libel, slander, incitement to violence, and so forth.) In a democracy those who oppose the policies of the government lose no civil rights and those who support its policies acquire thereby no civil rights. In a democracy minority opinion remains as untrammeled as majority opinion.

The importance of the creative role assigned to public opinion under democracy lies primarily in the fact that if opinion is free then the whole cultural life of man is free. If opinion is free, then belief is free and science is free and art and philosophy and all the variant styles and modes in which men manifest and develop their values and tastes and ways of living—always up to the limit where they endeavor by oppression or violence to deprive their fellowmen of these same prerogatives. Democracy alone assures the citadel of human personality against the deadly invasions of power. If only we could comprehend what this means we would never let our disappointments with the defects and weaknesses that the workings of democracy may reveal blind us to the intrinsic superiority of democracy over all other systems of government.

In direct and indirect ways democracy works for the enfranchisement of the mind and the liberation of the spirit. Taking as its premise the equal rights of men it is thereby committed to provide the conditions for the reasonable exercise of equal rights. Which means that democracy is committed to educate its citizens, all its citizens. Universal education has been a gift of democracy, free education not only in the sense that it is provided without fees but also in the sense that freedom of thought and of discussion is not balked by the demand of government that the teacher become an agent of its policies. It is true that education indoctrinates as well as informs. It is true that the schools of every country tend to inculcate the ways and the traditions of that country. But democracy does not, can not, believe in "thought control." It does not penalize those who think differently from the majority. It does not make government an arbiter of opinion. It leaves open all the avenues of dissent, so long as dissent does not commit itself to methods of violence.*

As soon as any government, calling itself democratic, sets up, directly or indirectly, any censorship of opinion it is betraying its cause. Democracy is the only system of government that trusts in its own persuasiveness, so that all the winds of doctrine have way within it. Democracy is the only system that has faith in the free mind. Democracy is the only system that does not make education the servant of power.

Democracy has therefore a more difficult goal than any other system. Because it trusts its citizens it makes higher demands on them, on their reason, on their integrity, on their faith, than does any other system. Actual democracies always lag, more or less, behind the standard they profess to accept. Their imperfections

* See on this point Chapter XI.

are often glaring. There are always strong interests that seek to pervert or corrupt the working of the democratic principle. And since propagandism is free there are always influences that spread hostile indoctrinations and prejudicial opinions in such wise as to weaken and threaten the solidarity on which the democratic structure must rest. The peoples need much preparation before they learn the ways of democracy, much experience and much education, and even when they have learned them they need to exercise much vigilance and devotion in order to retain them. But when we acknowledge these things we should recognize that the real defects of democracy lie not in its own principles, are not vices inherent in its very nature but instead the shortcomings and the misconceptions that prevent its principles from being fully implemented.

Unlike democracy, all other systems of government are flawed in their foundations, not merely in their superstructures. They all make function the servant of power, whereas democracy makes power the servant of function. In this respect they are all intrinsically *irrational.* They are all repressive, frustrating for the private advantage of a group or class the potentialities of human beings and the free development of community life. They all, in various degrees, subordinate or distort or suppress the creative spirit in man, the cultural spontaneity that expresses itself in free thought, in art, in literature, the activity above all others to which we owe the greatest, most distinctive, and most enduring achievements of humanity. It was no accident that the flowering of the genius of the race has taken place pre-eminently, though by no means exclusively, in countries that were moving towards or had already attained some form of democracy, in Greece, in Republican Rome, in the relatively free cities of the later Middle Ages, in England, in the countries of Western Europe, in the United States.

In a word, democracy liberates human nature. It confers increasingly, as it grows, those rights that, when men know how to use them, assure them the integrity and liberty of heart and mind in which they can advance toward new horizons. In this sense democracy humanizes society. All other forms of government do some inevitable distortion to humanity. Democracy sets itself out progressively to break the extrinsic and irrelevant barriers that cramp the potential worth of man. If sometimes it fails it is not because its program is faulty, but because men are not prepared to receive it or are too short-sighted and interest-blinded to accept it.

Part Two

———•—•———

THE VIOLENCE OF CHANGE

Chapter Seven

SOCIAL CHANGE AND SOCIAL

UNSETTLEMENT

Every social order, like every living thing, has forces working against it, threatening to destroy it. Some of these forces are present wherever a society exists. Others are peculiar to particular societies and particular times.

Every social order, the best as well as the worst, the most free as well as the most tyrannical, imposes certain restraints on strong human impulses. To begin with, it confines within prescribed limits two unruly urges, those concerned respectively with property and with sex. These urges are ever ready to rebel. Men covet the property of others, and the power that goes with property. No system, whether it be socialistic or grossly capitalistic, however equitable it be or however exploitative, however democratic or however tyrannical, can still the discontents of the eternally unsatisfied desire for more than is ours. Nor can any system make a treaty of peace with the "life force" of sex, such that its regulations, whatever they be, will not meet with restless violation and smouldering resistance.

Every social order cramps and balks men's imperious desires and no indoctrination is medicine strong enough to reduce them to faithful observance at all times. There is always frustration, and the bitterness of frustration is directed against the code and against the authority that administers the code. The resentment is often misdirected. Most codes, except the most tyrannical, give

more liberty than they deny. In the mythical "state of nature" men
would not be more free to follow their impulses and gratify their
desires. On the contrary, in the absence of law they would be controlled and frustrated more brutally and more completely than
they are under the rule of social custom and the legal code. The
theme of "civilization and its discontents," as expounded for example by Freud, is apt to ignore the more grim alternative.

But no such reflection can lessen the discontents that a social
order breeds. Moreover, there are always some kinds of inequality,
some disparities between the lot of man and man, of group and
group, some advantages possessed by some and coveted by others,
some differences in status, in the life chances, in esteem and prestige and power. The democratic order is committed to the re-
moval of irrelevant inequalities, inequalities arising from unequal
privilege and from unequal opportunity, but no order does or
even can make men equal in function, in position, or in authority.
There are always grievances and groups with grievances. There
are always leaders to exploit them, except where the iron fist of
autocracy is prompt to strike them down. There are always the
adventurous who seek advantage by rallying discontent and the
more adventurous who challenge the dogmas and the values of
the establishment.

Another source of unsettlement is the discrepancy between the
presumptive principles of the social order and the institutional
system that is presumed to embody them. This discrepancy goes
deeper than the discrepancy between the principles themselves
and the behavior of those who profess to follow them. In the
United States, for example, we go back to a Declaration that proclaims all men to be created equal and we have a Constitution
that forbids any abridgements of the privileges and immunities of
any citizens in any state of the Union, and specifically any denial
of the right to vote on account of race or color. Yet many millions
of citizens are habitually treated by the majority as inferiors or
outcasts and some states employ every device and subterfuge at
their command to abridge the right of certain minorities to vote.
This kind of contradiction is not peculiar to democratic states. In

varying degrees it exists everywhere. On the most gigantic scale it is exhibited within the Soviet Union, where the fundamental principles of the Constitution are not merely "abridged" but totally reversed by the character and policy of the government.

Our last example is of a quite exceptional nature. Leaving it aside for the present we conclude that there is always, under all forms of government, some ferment of opposition not merely to the particular administration in power but to the political system it represents. Normally the system can tolerate these discontents. It is normally well enough defended by the traditions it embodies, the loyalties it evokes, the indoctrinations it conveys, the inertia of the people, and the influence and power it wields. Only when particular conjunctures and particular crises greatly increase the number of the maladjusted and the discontented does real danger threaten.

Of all systems of government the democratic tolerates, with the least discomfort and the least friction, the more universal symptoms of resistance and discontent. For one thing, democracy is more flexible than other forms of government. Since it is directly responsive to public opinion it adjusts itself rather more easily to changing conditions and changing needs. Since it thrives on criticism it allows free vent to all grievances. Since it gives all men fundamental rights it liberates them from the most deadly of all frustrations, that which arises from the denial of the right to believe and think and communicate according to one's own heart and mind. Since it is friendly to individuality and widens the fields of opportunity it affords the adventurous most of the chances they seek. Its weakest side has been the failure to realize that the pursuit of life, liberty, and happiness requires some economic security as well as economic opportunity, especially in the age of "economic cycles," but this failure it is now doing more to overcome.

Hence in times of relative settlement, when peace and peaceful relations prevail between states, when no great intrusive forces of change disconcert the habits and hopes of men, democracy, once it is well established, keeps on advancing and makes new conquests. But in times of violent crisis democracy faces a special peril. The peril is greatest where the democratic heritage is recent and so has not taken deep root. But even in the old-established democracies the threat is far from negligible. When men become gravely insecure or profoundly disoriented they find it hard to maintain the balance, the tolerance, the trust in their fellow-men, the free attachment to free institutions, the sense of solidarity, that democracy demands. They become attuned to harsher disciplines, more irreconcilable conflicts, and more authoritarian leadership. They grow impatient and are more ready to resort to desperate policies and to put their trust in the ruthless man of power.

We have been living through times of surpassing changefulness. We are the heirs—or the victims—of a culminating series of socio-economic transformations. The ancient landmarks are all removed. The ancient signposts have all been obliterated. We march toward the future with no direction arrows from the past. This is the cumulative result of changes that began centuries ago but have passed all flood marks in our days. Movements and forces that emerged first in the period of the Renaissance have at length attained the fullness of their challenge.

In that period there began a new orientation of man to nature and to the understanding of nature. There was the first uneasy rejection of long-established traditions. With it went the questioning of old authority, and when some bold spirits began to question many others began to doubt. In politics there came the first pragmatic attacks on the hierarchy of power and class. "When Adam delved and Eve span, who was then the gentleman?" In religion some men were refusing to identify God with the *status quo,* were claiming to think for themselves, were refusing to recognize the unction of the priests, were beginning to hive off into dissident sects. The scheme of values was no longer secure. Reason or reasoning, reinforced by the first victories of science, was nibbling at the balances of faith.

In the later part of the eighteenth century the tempo of these changes was accelerated. The "age of enlightenment" had its own confident certainties, but these also, like the older traditions, were drawn into the vortex of fresh disturbances emanating mostly from the onset of the Industrial Revolution. The triumphant progress of technology had enormous impact on the most sacrosanct institutions. It brought new powers and a new distribution of power, more and more favorable to the lower ranks of the economic hierarchy. It stripped the household of ancestral duties and ancestral prerogatives. It reduced the family group to the minimum, breaking up the role of kinship. It took women into the factory and the office and worked great changes in their social and political status and more broadly in the relation of woman to man. It dissipated many ancient customs and stimulated many new kinds of organization. It brought about new relations and new clashes between peoples and states. It raised for large numbers, though at first with cruel partiality, the standard of living. It undermined the prerogatives of landownership. It extended the range of competition and, for a time at least, greatly increased its intensity. It created the new age of the market, which measured in precise and abstract units the value of all things that can be regarded as commodities. It led to a tremendous increase of specialization and to new and far more efficient modes of communication. It lengthened the expectation of life and made possible a tremendous growth of population. It inspired a new imperialism, the concomitant of ever-larger concentrations of capital. It made possible, and at last actual, the persistent trend of a declining birth-rate. It fostered new unities and it stimulated new divisions. Every schoolboy knows the story, but who can read its full meaning?

With these things came also nationalism, came the spread of democratic ideas and institutions, came the economic and educational opportunities that broadened the foundations of democracy. With them came also a new peril to democracy.

But on the whole the processes of change were favorable to democracy. The weakening of ancient authority, ancient prestige, the ancient hierarchy of class, the ancient privilege of land, was in its favor. Its extension was aided by the new distribution of power, by the new organization of labor, by the higher standard of living, by the swifter communication of ideas, by the greater mobility of occupation, by the growth of literacy and by the spread of a common culture through the whole range of each nationally minded people. There was indeed some endangering of democracy through the failure to reinterpret its demands under the new conditions. Democracy, unlike the more authoritarian principles, cannot afford to rest on tradition. If it does not look forward it decays. When it becomes hallowed it becomes untrue to itself. There was in the nineteenth century a tendency to a ritualistic acceptance of democracy as a tradition, so that even smug Toryism and complacent bureaucracy could claim to be holding aloft its banner. The antiquated identification of democracy with laissez-faire economics was congenial to various interests. They blandly interpreted the liberty of democracy as the liberty of capitalism, the liberty of their own interest groups. It was this tendency that gave some sting to the mockery of Lenin that "the capitalists have always called 'freedom' the freedom of profit for the rich, the freedom of the workers to die of hunger," or to the more urbane irony of Anatole France concerning the equality that allows the poor and the rich alike to sleep under the bridges.

Nevertheless, though private interests sought to capture, and thus indeed to kill, democracy, it was too vital to submit. Democracy advanced nearly continuously throughout the nineteenth century. The opportunities that are the logical consequences of its conferment of rights were provided more amply and more equally. The access to economic opportunity and to protection from the grave economic hazards of a capitalist system continued in considerable strength, though some democratic countries, and particularly the United States, were more laggard than others. In the countries of Western Europe democracy went on the heels of industrialization, gradually overcoming the resistance of feudal aristocracies and dynastic power-systems. Even in Russia the faint flush of a democratic dawn appeared, and there were evidences that the Orient was looking toward the light from the West.

Such was the situation until there broke into the changing world the most disintegrating of all precipitants of change—gigantic-scale, world-wide war, ending the hundred years of relative peace. The impact of war on a rapidly changing society was incalculably great. Alike the scale and the destructiveness of modern warfare are the consequence of the global interdependence that stems from modern technological advance, no less than of the new deadliness that technology has contributed to the weapons of war. The effects of this kind of war on a civilization so radically changed are quite unlike the effects of earlier wars. On the one hand it has utterly disrupted the complicated economic mechanism on which the welfare of uncounted millions depends. There is no such resumption of the established ways, no such gradual restoration of expectancies and habits of life, no such rebuilding of an old economy—except in a rare country that has escaped the direct fury of the conflict—as was normally the case after the wars of preceding centuries. On the other hand, in this age when authority has no fixed residence and when what faith exists has lost its reference to eternity, in this age when even in the days of peace many men found it hard to readjust their attitudes to the changing times, war has profound effects on the minds of men. Millions become "displaced persons," not in the physical sense but in the sense that they are driven out from the mental refuges of their former lives, from the familiar abode of their old responses and their old consolations. Modern war works violence on the minds of those who come near enough to it, the minds of the soldiers, of the bombed civilians, of the dispossessed, of the women who have lived nightmare lives within the vast areas over which its ravage passes, of the many who suffer precipitous changes of fortune. Its impact is naturally strongest on the countries that have suffered invasion, above all when defeat follows invasion, but the spread of its soul-devastating wings now reaches to the remote recesses of the earth.

Modern man has moved away from the spiritual anchorages of a simpler—shall we say a more primitive—world. He has, typically, no belief in an over-ruling Power or Providence that works in ways beyond man's understanding and somehow, in the end, brings good out of ill. Even when he professes a religious faith it remains, for the most part, remote from the actualities of his experience. He has no confidence in any hereafter where he will receive a blessed recompense for the trials and tribulations of his mortal life. He rejects the notion that his lot in life is set for him by any predestined scheme of things. Whatever order there is in the universe has nothing to do with him. He accepts no authority as anointed.

He is, as man always is, a social animal, dependent for spiritual as well as economic sustenance on his relation to the folk, *his* folk. But his attachments are less close, less secure. He is nationally minded, but the nation is too big and too diverse to give daily nourishment to his sense of belonging. He is a member of various organizations, but they are mostly ways-and-means organizations, pursuing a particular interest, embattled against other organizations that compete in the same field or stand for some counter-interest. They do not unite him to the whole—rather they separate him. His attachments to them are partial. Often they are perfunctory and temporary. He is no longer rooted in the life of the family or the life of the kin as were his forebears. His home is often a transient abode, perhaps a cell in the towering tiers of cells that make an apartment house, where he lives beside strangers —a neighborless man. His family is reduced to the conjugal group of husband, wife, and one or two young children. As the children grow they hive away. Most of the time the home itself is a place he leaves in the morning and returns to at night—a roosting place. His conjugal relations are not infrequently minimal or precarious, so that even this primary union is dissolved. The continuity of his present and his past is weak and at the mercy of circumstance.

Thus detached, thus insulated, modern man, the man of the industrial civilization of the West, makes as best he can some kind of adjustment to a world of change. What is left for him? He is thrown back on his own fortitude, his own initiative, his own interpretation, his own ability to weave a sustaining system of relationships. So far as he succeeds he has some compensations for his lack of stability. His individuality gets fuller play; he has more autonomy, more sense of adventure, more ambition, in some sense more freedom. In these respects he is the man to whom democracy is congenial, and his personality is responsive to the same forces that have shaped Western democracy. But while he may be adjusted to the less violent motions of social change he is all the more at the mercy of the sudden catastrophic changes that once and again have been breaking into our modern society. Of these the most calamitous by far is war, though a severe and prolonged economic crisis may have not dissimilar effects. Then the slender ties that attach him to society, the ties that support at the same time his sense of personal integrity, are likely to snap. And when that happens democracy is in grave peril. In our present-day world any catastrophic change is a body blow to democracy, and the most deadly of all these blows is delivered by war.

Chapter Eight

———•◆•———

RIFTS AND CLEAVAGES

Before we assess the impact on democracy of these more violent disturbances of our own times we shall consider a threat that has grown out of earlier and less abrupt processes of change. The changes we have here in view are the migrations of groups and the building up of larger more complex communities in which groups of different origin are mixed or juxtaposed. Many modern communities are in this sense "multigroup" societies, exhibiting a diversity of religion and culture and composed of elements drawn from different ethnic or racial stocks. Wherever this has occurred one group has tended to dominate another and to relegate it to an inferior position, and this dominance has overruled the democratic assumption of equal civil rights and of the citizen's liberty to participate in the affairs of the community. We are not referring here to the imperialistic control of a colonizing people over native populations, though in this respect also there has been witnessed often enough the spectacle of countries democratically ruled at home yet flagrantly violating all the premises of democracy abroad. Our immediate concern is with countries *within* which the disparagement of particular groups, because they have a different "national origin" or racial derivation, contradicts and undermines the democratic structure of government. This conflict exists, over a wider or a narrower range, in a number of countries. The most notable cases are those of the Union of South Africa and the United States of America. We shall confine our attention to the situation in the United States.

The existence of slavery in the United States had from the founding of the Republic been adverse to the development of democratic attitudes. Slavery was soon prohibited in the Northern states so that it became the "peculiar institution" of the South. The conditions under which slavery was finally abolished in the South were not such as to promote any change of attitude toward the man of color. Nor were the Northern states themselves inclined to remove the social and economic barriers that set the Negroes apart as a lower caste. In the nineteenth century, as immigrant groups from many countries arrived, disadvantaged as these were by linguistic obstacles and cultural differences and still more by their low economic status, there took shape an elaborate caste system, based not as in older lands on the inheritance of feudal stratifications but instead on distinction of origin, on the "distance" of the respective groups from the cultural standards and economic prerogatives of the dominant "Nordic" Whites—the distance of course being presumed to be greatest where color emphasized disparity. This caste system reached its full development in the great age of immigration that began in the eighties of the nineteenth century and was brought to a definite end in 1924.

The core of the system remained the distinction between the white man and the man of color. The principle of segregation was invoked against Negroes, Chinese, Japanese, Hindus, Filipinos, Latin-Americans, and American Indians. Less stringent restrictions impeded the economic opportunity and the social estimation of the peoples of the later migrations—Slavs, Eastern Europeans, Italians, and others. Finally, the ancient and peculiar discrimination to which the Jewish people are subject became more manifest as the waves of immigration carried considerable numbers who were fleeing the increased virulence of anti-Semitism in Russia and Southeastern Europe. All told, probably not less than forty million people within the United States were, by the time the Second World War broke, treated either as outcasts or, at best, as second-class citizens.

This anti-democratic stratification, with its strong quality of caste, remained seemingly unshaken in its major features until, say, 1940. Its flagrant violation of democratic principles elicited only an occasional protest and for the most part was wholly ignored. There was indeed a tendency to deny the very existence of social class in the United States. Apparently the system was rooted in the mores. Even the First World War had done nothing to crack it. There was then, as during the Second World War, the urgent need for manpower in industry but it did not open the avenues of higher grade employment to the Negro. Even in the federal civil service he made no gains. In fact, his exclusion from opportunity therein was even more complete when that war ended than when it began. The pattern of exclusion had hardened during the presidency of Taft, and the coming to power of the Democratic party under Wilson made the situation rather worse than before. Negroes were shut off from all except menial or custodial jobs. Nor did the New Deal mean at first any direct improvement in their lot. There was talk about the "new freedom" as well as about the New Deal, but for the most disprivileged groups it brought nothing but lip service. So far as federal employment was concerned the ancient art of politics worked full time to by-pass, shelve, or kill every application of the principles of human rights expounded on the platform. The time had not yet come when a President elected by the Democratic party could afford to affront the sentiment of the South.

As late as the year 1940 a superficial observer might have concluded that the system of caste discrimination was riveted in the social structure. Nevertheless in the preceding years a significant change of attitude had been proceeding that presently was to manifest itself in assaults on the entrenchments of group discrimination. One might, perhaps, have discovered early indications of the change in the reversal by the Supreme Court of its previous refusal to apply the Fourteenth Amendment to the protection of citizens against infringements of civil rights by states or local government—a change of attitude registered in the case of *Gitlow* v. *New York* in 1925. Moreover, the National Association for

the Advancement of Colored People was becoming active, seeing
to it that strategic cases were brought before the Supreme
Court. The denial by Texas and Virginia of the Negro's right to
vote in the primaries was declared to be unconstitutional under
the Fourteenth Amendment. Perhaps a sign of the changing times
was the fact that even in the Southern states the number of Negroes enrolled in high schools more than doubled between 1920
and 1930, with a corresponding increase in public school expendi-
tures on Negro education. There was some evidence too of a
greater tendency to question and to protest against the denial of
opportunity to the Negro. But the caste system as a whole remained intact. And in the depression years the right of the Negro
to vote in the Southern states received a setback from new decisions of the Supreme Court.

The first conclusive evidence of the cracking of the system was
the establishment in 1941 of the Fair Employment Practice
Committee. The FEPC had no legal existence; it was set up by
executive order, not by congressional action. It was a wartime
measure applicable to war industries, with its activities balked at
many points by strong resistance both inside and outside the
Administration. Indeed it would probably not have come into
existence except for the "march on Washington" organized by
Negro groups. Here was the modest and yet very significant beginning of a great change. From then on the forces of discrimination
were put on the defensive and since then they have suffered defeats on every front. In the "department service" of the Federal
Government, while the total number of Negroes employed increased fourfold between 1938 and 1944, the number classified as
professional or semiprofessional increased ninefold and the number occupying various clerical ratings was multiplied by twenty-
five. In private employment important advances were also registered. There was a notable upsurge into the hitherto scarcely
accessible grades of skilled work, of clerical work, and to a lesser
extent of professional work. The number of female Negroes in
clerical occupations was half of one per cent of the total of clerical
workers in 1920 and rose to nearly five per cent by 1947. The

movement was not halted by the change from wartime to peace-
time conditions. Even when signs of a recession began in 1949
there were not the seriously adverse repercussions on Negro employment that might have been anticipated. At the same time
Negroes were gaining admission into many previously closed
unions. They were being admitted along with Whites into various
housing developments, and the restrictive agreement received a
setback from a decision of the Supreme Court. In nearly every
area of the national life, from the representation of the United
Nations to the arenas of professional baseball, Negroes began to
play a role from which they had hitherto been excluded.

The change in question was part of a broader movement, in
which the various groups previously disprivileged on grounds of
national origin or of race were approaching nearer to equality of
opportunity. The most obvious sign of it was the passage in a number of states of acts that forbade ethnic or racial discrimination by
employers of any kind or by trade unions. Legislation of this sort
was a new development. It is true that there already existed quite
a few laws prohibiting discrimination in admission to public resorts, restaurants, schools, to public services and facilities of various kinds, but these laws were largely inoperative and seldom invoked. The new laws contained provision not only for enforce-
ment but also for standing commissions to see that they were
carried into effect. Were they workable? Grave doubts were expressed about it. Probably many legislators voted for the new laws
in order not to lose the votes of minority groups but without believing the law would be of much effect. The first act of this kind
was passed in the state of New York in 1945. It was speedily
followed by similar acts in Massachusetts, New Jersey, Connecti-
cut and Rhode Island; in the Far West Oregon, Washington,
and New Mexico followed suit, while a number of other states
began to give the matter some consideration.

All this happened in the space of a very few years. There can
be no question of the change in the climate of opinion. There was
still strong resistance. The advance was very uneven. There were

industries that, except in states where the new legislation prevailed, maintained a "lily-white" policy. Craft unions clung to
their discriminatory rules. Professional organizations limited the
entrance of the groups subject to discrimination. Educational institutions kept their doors half closed to the same groups, where
they were not wholly shut. Everywhere there continued to be
restrictive agreements in residential areas. Large parts of the
country seemed little affected by the changes evidenced elsewhere.
The South made practically no relaxation of its denial of occupa-
tional opportunity. The ancient and obdurate prejudice against
the Jews remained strong, although the more clamant expressions
of anti-Semitism were stilled. As for the anti-discrimination laws,
they were applied only in the mildest manner. The Commissions
responsible for carrying them out listened to complaints from
aggrieved applicants for employment, called obviously offending
employers to hearings, obtained promises of reform from them,
and in no case resorted to the courts.

In short, it was a change, not a revolution. It came at a critical
time in world history and in part at least it was an answer to the
challenge of the time. In two world wars the United States had
entered the conflict under the guise of a champion of democracy.
During the Second World War it took over its new character as
the greatest of world powers, with only one other contender
for that title. That other power was dedicated to a totally different, a wholly contradictory, philosophy of government. It claimed
that its own system was the true and only genuine kind of democracy. And in particular it claimed that under its system the discrimination of group against group, of dominant groups over disprivileged groups, was entirely abolished. It claimed that the exploitation of group by group was inherent in the false democracy
of capitalist society. Under this banner it carried on the most intensive propaganda to win over to its side the peoples of the earth.
Whatever may be said for its other claims and charges there was
a sting in its accusation about the manner in which the United
States subordinated and exploited ethnic groups, above all its

colored groups. Here was a most glaring denial of the principles of democracy by the country that claimed to be its greatest exponent and champion.

The challenge thus presented was reinforced by the new situation in which the United States found itself during the war and after its end. Its new role as a world power brought it into closer relations with the Orient. The rise of the sense of nationality in China and India and Burma and Indonesia and Malaysia and the Philippines accentuated the resentment of these peoples against the brand of inferiority placed upon them in the United States. Its leadership in world affairs was embarrassed also by the emotions aroused in all Latin-American states over the indignities their nationals suffered when they set foot in "the land of the free." The proclamation of the "good neighbor" policy could hardly be very effective when the neighbor's neighbor was barred from eating in the same restaurants or sleeping in the same hotels.

At the same time there were deep-moving processes of change within the United States that promoted a change of attitude and of policy. American confidence in the merits of a rather hard-shelled economic individualism, already weakened by the growing concentration of economic power, received a staggering blow in the Great Depression. The measures for greater social security that followed, under the name of the New Deal, indicated more than a temporary expedient to tide over a period of distress. The increasing support given to these measures, the changing character of party programs, and the continued dominance of a party proclaiming itself to be "left of center," witnessed to a new orientation of public opinion, a growing sense of social responsibility, an increasing rejection among the masses of the people of the old individualistic tradition. As time went on this change of attitude began to invade the area of inter-group discrimination and prejudice. Certain historical factors gave it further stimulation. The practical cessation of immigration undermined the difference of economic status between the immigrant groups and the more established groups. It became harder to identify the Eastern Europeans or the Southern Italians as "hewers of wood and drawers of water."

They, too, were rising in the world. Another significant change was the large migration of Negroes to the Northern cities, accompanied in its later stages by the spread of certain Northern industries into the South. The Negro was ceasing to be tied to the land, in a kind of peonage. And in the Northern cities he could organize and he could vote, and in time he began to learn that thereby he could make his voice heard and his influence felt. All in all, considerable changes in the distribution of power were occurring in the United States.

The convergence of these changes has been registered in the growing uneasiness with which people all over the United States have begun to view the discriminatory practices that had taken such hold on the community. Hundreds of organizations have been formed for the purpose of combating or of mitigating these practices. Definite advances have been achieved in the direction of greater economic opportunity. Racial barriers to the admission of Orientals have been somewhat reduced and the restrictions on their naturalization have been for the most part removed. Educational disabilities are under constant attack. In Northern colleges exclusive fraternities have begun to include Negroes in their membership. An order for the establishment of a policy of racial equality in the army has been issued. The Supreme Court has declared that restrictive housing covenants are unenforceable by legal processes. Even in the South a Negro ventures to run for public office and to appeal for White support. Many other instances could be cited to show that a highly significant change has been taking place in public opinion and is being reflected in social policy.

These gains are still most partial victories, but they unquestionably reveal a trend. The United States is becoming aware of the most fatal defect in its democratic armor, one that has left it exceedingly vulnerable both at home and abroad. It would be rash to claim that the deadly peril has been overcome. There is still the racial segregation in the South and there are the racial ghettos of the North. Assumptions of ethnic superiority are still widely prevalent throughout the country. Educational handicaps are maintained by various devices and the entry to the professions is still restricted. The avenues of economic opportunity are still blocked at many points. And there remains, seemingly undiminished in its extent though perhaps less virulent in its expression, the ancient tradition of prejudice against the Jewish people, a prejudice that seems to carry with it a peculiar nemesis.

The peril to democracy arising from the discrimination and prejudice against particular groups is still most serious. The hopeful thing is that there has been growing among the American people an uneasy if inadequate recognition of the contradiction between the habit of discrimination and the goals to which they are committed at home and abroad.

Chapter Nine

---·•·---

THE PERIL OF GROUP ANARCHY

We have pointed out that the democratic way is disturbed and shaken by abruptly intrusive or catastrophic changes and above all by the unmeasured destructiveness of modern war. War in our times reduces all the potentialities of a civilized people to two stark alternatives, maimed survival or ruin—survival through the greater destruction it inflicts on the enemy than the enemy, on it, or the unmitigated ruin of defeat. The fury of its destructiveness and the sudden thrust that constricts the hearts of men and reduces their minds to a far lower level of aspiration have a deteriorating effect on democratic attitudes, just as for the time they practically negate the resort to democratic processes. In particular, the condition of war and still more the aftermath of war tend to conspire with two disintegrative tendencies that develop within modern democracy, though these are usually held in check by the counter-forces of the democratic system.

One is the dissipation of the sense of common interest—the "general will"—into the particularist interests of competing or conflicting groups, highly organized for the detached advantage of each. The other is the weakening of the *individual's* sense of social solidarity and thus of social obligation not only to the larger community but even to his own group. No longer disciplined by the strong sanctions of old-time authority, no longer enveloped in an all-pervading atmosphere of common customs and common standards, the individual is under particular temptation, which the educative influences of democracy may be unable to counteract, to give free vent to his egoistic impulses and to regard society as nothing but the arena of private interests.

It was Rousseau who first depicted this latter tendency as a peculiar peril of democracy:

> Each individual may as a man, exercise a will at variance with, or different from, that general will to which, as a citizen, he contributes. His personal interest may dictate a line of action quite different from that demanded by the interest of all. The fact that his own existence as an individual has an absolute value, and that he is, by nature, an independent being, may lead him to conclude that what he owes to the common cause is something he renders of his own free will, and he may decide that he does less harm to his fellows by leaving the debt unpaid than he would to himself by making the necessary surrender. Regarding the moral entity constituting the state as an abstraction of reason because it is not a man, he might enjoy his rights as a citizen without fulfilling at the same time his duties as a subject, and the resultant injustice might grow until it brought ruin on the body politic.

Both of these tendencies, the detached egoism of the group and the detached egoism of the individual, undermine the free consensus, the uncompulsive unauthoritative solidarity that is the basis and the peculiar virtue of democracy. When aggravated by the insecurities and disorientations of times of crisis these tendencies may cleave asunder the social fabric. Group egoism then becomes group anarchy, a confused and bloodless civil war—though when it takes the special form of class war it may end in bloody revolution. It is the breeding-ground of extremist doctrines that expose the nakedness of power, of ruthless creeds and embittered ideologies. Among its brood are fascism and modern communism. Under the same conditions individual egoism in turn takes its extremer form, a form that until recently had received no name and still lacks one in the English speech. We shall call it

anomy.[1] It is the fulfilment of the process of desocialization, the re-
treat of the individual into his own ego, the sceptical rejection of
all social bonds. It too has its appropriate ideologies, such as
dadaism in art and existentialism in philosophy. In politics it
logically attaches itself to doctrines of the irresponsible elite. It is
interested in the techniques of power, more than in any goals to
which power may be the means.

These, then, are the two directions, the road of group anarchy
and the road of personal anomy, along which, in an age of change,
are driven the more unstable minds under the impact of grave
crisis. They both lead to the same end of the road. They both are
perils to democracy. Let us examine them more closely.

The first direction, that of group anarchy, of group detachment
from the sense of community, has been noted by various writers
of our time. Some have even gone so far as to maintain that the
modern specialization of functions and interests and the consequent growth of great interest groups and of vast and powerful
organizations devoted exclusively to their advancement, has destroyed the very basis of social life, dissipating the loyalties and
emotional commitments that unite men into true communities.
We need not accept this pessimistic conclusion in order to perceive the genuine threat pronounced to be fatal by these conservative thinkers. They can muster impressive evidences. The mo-
nopoly-seeking corporation, the patent-engrossing cartel, the price-
fixing syndicate, the lobbying pressure group, the ubiquitous
propaganda agency, exert on every side their irresponsible power
and influence. The business of a very large number of men, directors, managers, agents, politicians, advertisers, lawyers, and so on,
has become wholly that of promoting the special interests or
prerogatives of some group apart from any relation to the public
interest.

It is an evil most manifest under a capitalistic system, but it is
rooted in the magnitude and complexity of modern economic and

[1] The French name, "anomie," taken over from the sociologist Emile Durkheim,
is beginning to be used in English and should now be given English form.

political organization. In one form or another it is likely to inhere in any technologically advanced society, with its specialization of function. The private interest of the specialized functionary will vary with the nature of the system. In the more competitive capitalistic structure he will seek primarily to maximize his economic advantage, without regard for the interest of the public. In the socialistic structure he will seek primarily to maximize bureaucratic security and power and authority, no less at the expense of the public. The evil is indigenous in the scale of organization.

The central problem of modern government springs from two facts, both of which are the result of the processes of specialization. One fact is the diversity of groups, and thus of interests, that exists within the framework of government. The other is the patchwork distribution of power that develops as these diverse groups organize to further their particular interests. The dominant aspect of modern specialization is the specialization of *function*. Every functional group, once it becomes organized, gains a very important power, the power to give or withhold that function according as its own terms are met or rejected. There are, it is true, some conditions that limit the exercise of this power, but, on the whole, the power itself inheres, at least in degree, in all organizations that are not merely instruments of government.

This specialization of function works significantly on the outlook of men. They see things more and more from one aspect, the aspect of the function they respectively fulfil. This is true alike of scholars and of artists, of professional men and of business men. The scholar comes to think his own specialty more important, as well as more engrossing, than other areas of knowledge. The narrower his field, the more he tends to confine himself within it. In his case this attitude is relatively independent of economic interest. When, however, as is more generally the case, the economic incentive potently supplements the functional prejudice the organized functional group doubly overestimates its own *relative* importance in the scheme of things. It employs the power of organization to make excessive demands on the total economy. Inevitably it subordinates the general welfare to the special interest for which it stands.

The new distribution of power in the specialized society makes impossible any return to the older class state. Under earlier conditions one class was supreme, primarily a land-owning class. With this one "function" went power and privilege and authority. There was little effective challenge until the organization of function accompanied the specialization of function. When this happened social power ceased to have any correspondence with prior prestige. No upper social class could retain its former prerogatives. It would indeed seem as though, under modern conditions, only two types of state are possible. One is democracy, the other is dictatorship. Dictatorship meets the problem by "co-ordinating" all organizations under its own absolute power, destroying their autonomy and relying on force and monopolized indoctrination to prevent any resistance. Democracy meets the problem by admitting the autonomy of functional organizations, subject to the consensus of the people as a whole, the voting public, respecting the limits within which that autonomy may be exercised without danger to the common welfare.

Both systems have their risks, but it is obvious that if democracy really *works* it is a better system, since unmitigated force and fear arrest the creative processes of social experience. But the assumption of democracy is that the sense of the public interest will move the majority of the public and that it will on the whole over-ride the encroachments and aggressions of particular private interests. If this assumption should prove false, democracy must, in the longer run, break down. Democracy cannot long coexist with group anarchy.

In democratic countries, and notably in the United States, there have been not a few political theorists who understand democracy in much narrower terms. Ever since the founding of the Republic there has been controversy between those who, like Jefferson, regarded democracy as sustained by the sense of the common interest and those who, like Hamilton and Madison, tended to regard it as resting essentially on the compromise of particular interests. The latter conception has perhaps received additional impetus from the stress laid on "checks and balances" in the Constitution of the United States. It has been much in vogue in recent times. One of the most explicit statements of it is offered in A. F. Bentley's *The Process of Government.* He rejects the notion of the "general will" altogether. The very "substance of democracy" is a system of opposing group pressures. Government simply registers the adjustment or compromise of these pressures, the resultant attained through the conflict of various pressures of varying strength.

There is a measure of truth in the doctrine of Bentley and his school. It is obviously true that particular interests are always active, always driving to make government their servant. It is true that in the conflict of these interests some kind of mere compromise is not infrequently reached. It is true also that the nature of the general welfare itself is construed differently by different groups and that *one* explanation of the difference is the readiness with which men identify the public interest with their own particular interests. Formally, then, the processes of democratic decision may well appear as nothing more than the accommodation of opposing forces along some diagonal of compromise.

But to stop here would be to leave out the vital element of democracy. It would be to leave out the sense of community that is operative in the hearts and minds of every people, the sense of community to which democracy alone gives full and free expression. It is implied in the resort to the electorate, in the willingness to accept the majority verdict, in the adhesion to a whole code of laws most of which aroused controversy at the time of enactment, in the constant appeal of every leader and of every party to the common cause, however biased may be the particular interpretation of it, in the longer trends of public opinion revealing as they do that the same influences pervade a whole people, in the evocation of patriotic impulses and endeavors when manifest danger threatens the commonweal, in the belief of the people in its unity, in its inheritance, in its common future. If we leave out these things we leave out the meaning of democracy. For democracy alone places its whole reliance on these things. They constitute indeed the "general will." Without them we have group anarchy, the dissolution of democracy.

Group interests will not suffice. Democracy can accept them, can use them, so long as beyond them there lives the abiding sense of community. Let us consider again what happens where this cement of democracy begins to weaken, to crack.

In a complex society all functions, all groups, all services are thoroughly interdependent. They are all so geared together that a hold-up or interruption at any point will cause a serious disturbance of the whole economy and if prolonged may threaten its very existence. Those who control any great industrial organization, whether as industrial managers or as labor leaders, have thus a tremendous engine of power. Even a relatively small function may be essential, directly or indirectly, to the operation of the entire system. If, for example, tugboat workers or elevator men or street cleaners or teamsters withhold their services until their demands are met they are in effect saying: "We shall paralyze the economy by degrees unless you yield." This power has done signal service in raising the standards of the working people and counteracting the exploitation from which they have suffered, often grievously, in the past. But the weapon has become so formidable that unless those who possess it are animated by a high sense of social responsibility it degenerates into an intolerable menace.

On the other hand there is a less obvious but no less real menace in the irresponsible use of managerial power. It is an abuse of power to restrict, for purposes of corporate advantage, the supply of any important commodity, such as steel or other construction materials, to peg the prices of a commodity when costs are falling, to drive competitors out of business in a price war in order to control the market afterwards, to buy up serviceable patents in order to prevent their development, or to use any of the numerous devices for manipulating stock capital for the greater wealth and power of the management and to the detriment of the investor, the worker, and the public. When such practices are defended under the ironic name of "free enterprise" the whole system so named loses repute. The defenses of democracy are still further weakened when government joins hands with exploiting groups or corporations. This has happened often enough in countries calling themselves democracies, and not least in the United States. For example, the state of Louisiana, a flagrant offender in this respect, gave to a particular corporation a monopoly of the slaughterhouse business in certain parishes of New Orleans, thus driving many butchers out of business—and the Supreme Court of the United States decided, not once but several times, that this kind of governmental buccaneering was not contrary to the provisions of the Fourteenth Amendment.

Organization is power; great organization is great power, and even in democracies it is usually, in the last resort, the power of a very few. The particular interest of any organization is likely, if given full play, to invade at some point the public domain. The particular interest of its executives is not in all respects the interest of the organization, but it is greatly advanced whenever the organization increases its resources, extends its influence, or gains some victory over other organizations. Thus the managerial group is under constant temptation to magnify the organization and disregard the community, to maximize function and minimize service.

A similar spirit of detachment operates on a lower level, often in ways that pass the bounds of legality. Here, for example, are three items taken from the New York press on a single day in November, 1948:

(1) An investigation showed that automobile dealers in the United States had, outside of fair business practices, mulcted the buyers of new cars during seven months of a "sellers' market" out of four hundred and fifty million dollars, through such devices as the under valuation of trade-ins, the insistence on the purchase of unwanted extras, the charging of premiums above list prices, and so forth.

(2) It was reported that the leaders of a certain union signed an agreement with the employers, pronouncing it "a fine agreement." A rival for leadership of the union organized a wild-cat strike,

whereupon the union president made a quick about-face and to save his own position made the strike official.

(3) It was reported, with circumstantial detail, that a group of racketeers with trade union connections had for a number of years been "high-jacking" consignments of goods at the New York docks, through an elaborate system of collusion involving false billing, false weighing, and false loading, thus taking tolls amounting to many millions of dollars every year.

We are of course in no position to guarantee the accuracy of these particular reports, but there is abundant evidence that behavior of this sort is rampant and ramifies deep into our multi-group industrial society. Apart from the direct evils it brings, it loosens the fabric of democratic consensus. In the language of Rousseau, "such injustice would in its progress cause the ruin of the body politic."

——— ◆ ◆ ———

Chapter Ten

DESCENT TO ANOMY

Let us look next at *anomy,* the other malady of democratic man that becomes most virulent in times of crisis and turbulent change, the breakdown of the individual's sense of attachment to society, to all society. Anomy is not simply lawlessness. A gangster or a pirate or a mere law-evading rogue is not as such, indeed is not likely to be, anomic. He has his own code of law against law and is under strong sanctions to obey it. He need not be the victim of that inner detachment, of that cleavage between the real self and the projected self, of that total rejection of indoctrinated values that characterizes the anomic person. Anomy signifies the state of mind of one who has been pulled up from his moral roots, who has no longer any standards but only disconnected urges, who has no longer any sense of continuity, of folk, of obligation. The anomic man has become spiritually sterile, responsive only to himself, responsible to no one. He derides the values of other men. His only faith is the philosophy of denial. He lives on the thin line of sensation between no future and no past.

In any times particular individuals may fall into anomy. It happens when sensitive temperaments suffer without respite a succession of shocks that disrupt their faith. And not a few men have temporary moods that resemble anomy, periods when the spirit of denial rules them, after they have experienced some grave bafflement. But there are times of profound disturbance when whole groups are exposed to the malady. The soldiers in Mailer's novel, *The Naked and the Dead,* talk the language of anomy. They have been torn in youth from their environments, their careers, their dreams, their hopes, to face laborious tedium and the ugliest forms of death. They have been bereft of the sustaining ways of their culture. They are thrust back on the immediate needs and demands of each perilous hour. The present offers nothing but sensations; there are periods of boredom and drudgery, and then they are alone with nature and sudden death. So they use the language of sensation—there is nothing else to express. It means little but there is nothing else to mean. The livid, gory, sexy words they utter soon convey precisely nothing, nothing but the denudation they feel. For them, however, for those who survive, there is a return to nearly all the things they have lost. For most of them anomy wears away in their restoration to their society. But there are others, the hopelessly displaced, the totally uprooted, the permanently insecure, those who need the support of authority and have lost it without hope of recovery, the over-sophisticated who find that the challenges of life cannot be met by sophistication— among such people anomy takes full command.

Anomy is a state of mind in which the individual's sense of social cohesion—the mainspring of his morale—is broken or fatally weakened. In this detachment of the anomic person from social obligation his whole personality is injured. He has lost the *dynamic unity* of personality. The anomic fall into various types, though we do not have so far the psychological researches necessary for the adequate classification of these types. We can, however, broadly distinguish the following.

First, there are those who, having lost altogether, or in great measure, any system of values that might give purpose or direction to their lives, having lost the compass that points their course into the future, abandon themselves to the present, but a present emptied of significance. They resort, in other words, to a sophisticated cynicism, by aid of which they rationalize their loss. They live by the hour, seeking immediate gratification on whatever level it is available. They tend to be sensationalists and materialists. It is their defense against the ghosts of perished values.

Second, there are those who, having lost their ethical goals, having no longer any intrinsic and socialized values to which they can harness their drive to action, transfer this drive to extrinsic values instead, to the pursuit of means instead of to the pursuit of ends beyond them, and particularly to the pursuit of power, so far as that lies within their reach. It has been claimed that there is a "strain toward anomy" in modern capitalistic society, with its emphasis on competitive success measured by the purely extrinsic standard of money-making. There can be little doubt that engross-ment in the competitive struggle, especially when it is carried on under the aegis of the "soul-less body-less" corporation, diverts men from the search for intrinsic satisfactions and erodes their recognition of the common interests of their society, the inclusive more abiding interests that bind men in the responsible fellowship of their community. At the same time, the experience of the past two generations suggests that it requires the violence of change, the deeper perturbations that disorient and displace men from their former ways, their former goals, their former faiths, to bring anomy to its full being, and in particular this second type of anomy. Those who exhibit it tend to be domineering, sadistic, ruthless, irascible, vain, inherently destructive. Unlike the first type, they live for a future, they have objectives that bind today to the further tomorrow, but these objectives are self-centered, ego-glorifying, bereft of social obligation. Often they profess adher-ence to some intrinsic faith or value, but primarily because that profession enhances their private designs. They are then like Machiavelli's prince, who must appear to be religious and high-minded if he is to retain his prestige and power. Moreover, they make the creeds of other men the instruments of their own ag-grandisement, the utilitarian myths of their authority. On another level they are racketeers, buccaneers of industry or finance, un-principled exploiters of whatever position, privilege, or power they acquire. All men or nearly all men cherish their private interest and frequently enough they allow it to overcome their public obligation. But they are restrained within certain limits set by loyalties of one kind or another, and when they transgress they are conscious of dereliction. But the truly anomic man has no limit short of necessity and no conscience that is more than expediency.

Third, we may distinguish a type of anomy that is characterized above all by a fundamental and tragic insecurity, something that cuts deeper than the anxieties and dreads that beset other men. It is the insecurity of the hopelessly disoriented. They have lost the ground on which they stood, the ground of their former values. Usually it happens when they have lost also their former environment, their former connections, their social place, their economic support. In the profoundest sense they are "displaced persons." The displacement, however, may not be physical. There is, for example, the social alienation of those who feel themselves rejected and become the victims of a persecution complex. This is perhaps the bitterest of all forms of anomy. There is a crushing sense of indignity, of exclusion, of injustice, of defeat, arousing feelings of intense hate, counter-aggressiveness, total revulsion from things as they are, sometimes accompanied by unquiet introspection and self-torture.

This cursory review is intended to suggest types, not to classify them. In any event there is a considerable overlapping of attributes between our types. We should also remember that many people approach the full bent of anomy in various degrees. As we have already suggested, the conditions of our civilization create some predisposition to it and when our kind of civilization is racked by abrupt and violent change anomy grows rampant. Anomy is a disease of the civilized, not of the simpler peoples. As Durkheim pointed out, one index of anomy is the number of suicides, and suicide is much more frequent among the civilized.

It is noteworthy that modern doctrines of violent social change are initiated by those who have at least a tendency to anomy. Let us take for example the case of Karl Marx. He was from his early youth subjected to some of the conditions that breed anomy. His family belonged to the rabbinical elite in Germany. While he was still an infant his father, to the general surprise, announced his conversion to the Protestant Evangelical Church. This was the cause of a bitter dispute between his father and his mother. In the end, when Karl was six years old, his father had his way, and Karl, along with the six other children of the family, was baptized into the new faith. We know from modern studies how deeply disturbing it is to the mind of a child to have his first indoctrinations shattered by a "culture clash" on the hearth. The secret churning of the young boy's mind was the first preparation of the revolutionist-to-be, greatly heightening that sense of aloofness and disorientation that is the lot of many a Jewish boy in a society that stupidly clings to its hoary prejudices. The first obvious effect on Karl Marx was his loathing of all religions.

He grew into an impetuous, irascible, opinionated, and still idealistic youth. Then his ambitions suffered a series of reverses and frustrations. At this stage he fell in with the "communist rabbi," Moses Hess. He was ripe for the new gospel. He embraced it avidly, inclining at first toward the French socialists but soon repudiating and scorning them to assert his own truly scientific brand. It was the culmination of a process that began in the disorientation of childhood. Marx had become completely alienated from the society in which he lived, not its economic order particularly but its whole being and all the culture it nourished. In the background of his mind there flickered visions of an ideal society. But his love of the ideal was pale and distant compared with his hatred of the actual. He turned early to dreams of power, of lonely mastery. He was at enmity with the world. He denounced with incredible bitterness his own best friends the moment they ventured to question in any way his authority.

A man may condemn the society in which he lives without being himself anomic. But only if he is sustained by the engrossing vision of a better society, only if he is working to hasten the coming of some "new Jerusalem," only if he lives in fellowship with some brotherhood of the faithful who share his vision, only, in the last resort, if he is already, prophetically, a member of the society for which he yearns. There are those who believe the main inspiration of Marx was just some such redemption of mankind, that he was filled with the vision of a world in which men would be liberated from exploitation and injustice, from the gross oppression of every form of power. To the present writer that seems a mistaken interpretation. In the voluminous writings of Marx there are only one or two most fleeting references to "the good society." There is no evidence that he really cared for his fellowmen. He never uses kindly language except for those who looked upon him as their infallible leader. He hated those of his own party who showed any independence of thought. He was venomous toward all whom he could not dominate.

Marx focused his sharp intelligence on the worst sore of the society he hated. A new industrial system had been growing up. It was being exploited with callous disregard for the welfare of the workers. In the "dark Satanic mills," as the poet Blake called them, men, women, and young children labored endlessly long days, under the worst conditions, for subsistence wages or less. There were riots and threats of revolution. The French Revolution had shown how a class system could be overthrown. Here Marx found his opportunity. With immense vigor and remarkable propagandistic skill he proclaimed the inevitable victory of the proletariat. Marx had never mixed with any proletarians. He was himself a bourgeois. He never showed any interest in proletarians as human beings—only as a class. As he himself said, he found in the proletariat the "material weapon of philosophy," of his philosophy, of his revenge on society, of his triumph. He was the wrathful divider. The "bourgeoisie" became the fixed objective of his hate, the source of all evil. He identified it with the society that had rejected him. It was anathema. He devoted his being to its destruction.

The presence of anomy in modern society is evidenced by the spread of violently divisive doctrines, doctrines of all-or-nothing, doctrines that loudly preach a reactionary or a revolutionary authoritarianism, doctrines that appeal to men not as human beings but as de-individualized masses in motion. The anomic and near-anomic persons of the second and third types are particularly prone to such doctrines. For they offer a congenial release from anomy, a drastic remedy for its bitterness and frustration, a refuge from its insecurity, a means of reconciling its destructive tendencies with its secret need for social reintegration.

All these doctrines are enemies of democracy. They reject its tolerance, its acceptance of difference, its respect for the individual, its faith in the healing processes of free opinion. The anomic man has lost the balance of social health, mostly through no fault of his own. In his alienation he seeks a quick and false prescription. The anomic who cannot be masters are often ready to be slaves. They cry out for the superman to save them, for some equivalent of a Providence, a God, the ineluctable authority who will end their alienation by saying, "I command you to follow," making his command ring with the magic of a lost obligation.

What then can democracy do to meet these two perils that threaten it in this age of violent change—group anarchy and individual anomy? We remarked in passing that we should not blame the anomic for their plight; they are suffering from a disease incident to our civilization. The remark may seem at best a truism—of what other social ailment might not the same be said? But it was said to call attention to the proper ways in which democracy can safeguard itself against these dangers. When we seek to heal a social ailment—or a physical one—we should always treat it as a disease and not as a sin. Unfortunately we often proceed on the latter assumption, as we have been doing, for example, in our "denazification" policies, with mostly unhappy consequences. To protect democracy against anomy or against group anarchy we must endeavor to get at and to remove their causes.

In the first place we should realise that all our efforts to protect democracy against these and other dangers are wholly futile unless we can protect it first against the catastrophe of war. For war has now become so immeasurably ruinous that the shaken and impoverished survivors would be driven to desperate measures that might be fatal to the very existence of democracy. Therefore while we still possess the inestimable spiritual heritage of democracy we must assure it against the very possibility of war, showing an alertness and a forethought that in the past two generations the democratic world most deplorably failed to show.

To achieve this end democracy must be strong in its quality as democracy, not only in its arms. The spiritual weakness of democracy is the strength of its enemies. In some respects we still make only a pretence at democracy. Ask the Mexican-Americans within our borders, whom we do not permit to sit at the same table with our noble Nordics. Ask the Negroes, whom we segregate as pariahs, so that we may not be contaminated by the social presence of a lower caste. Ask the Jewish people, who cannot live in the same hotels, sometimes cannot even be treated in the same hospitals as their democracy-loving fellow-Americans. Ask the Eastern Europeans, who are still frequently treated as second-class citizens, especially if their names have a Slavic sound. Ask the Chinese among us, the Japanese, the Filipinos, the Hindus— and remember that by our treatment of these people we are betraying our democracy before the greater part of the human race; remember also that the Orient is now stirring to new political life and that its decision between democracy and dictatorship will profoundly affect our future and the future of all mankind. Ask these questions, remember these things, and you must see that *our* failure to be true to *our* democracy is in the last resort the main reason why democracy is in danger.

The diseases of group anarchy and of personal anomy are peculiarly incident to modern democracies. The unfree systems are authoritarian; by authority and by sheer compulsion they suppress such manifestations. Democracy places responsibility in the individual and in the group—it asks their free allegiance, their free cooperation. But it must on that account assure its citizens the conditions in which they can exercise their freedom. It must guard them from haunting economic insecurity or their civic freedom becomes a mockery. It must guard them against the rank prejudice that cuts them off from the equal partnership of democratic society. Otherwise democracy will breed the seeds of its own destruction.

Lastly, it must make its own meaning, its own philosophy, its own spirit, positive and vital. It cannot rest in the outworn liberalism that never rose above the negative of non-intervention. No vague negative faith can meet men's needs in this age where dogmatic authoritarian creeds deride the democratic ideal, and promise men, however falsely, a greater security and a greater reward. Democracy must become self-conscious of its own worth. Here we reach a theme that needs our most earnest attention.

Part Three

———•◦•———

THE ENEMY FROM WITHOUT

Chapter Eleven

———— •◆• ————

THE MASK OF DEMOCRACY

In these days a new peril has arisen against the whole historical tradition of democracy. An enemy that disguises its deep hatred under the cloak of the thing it hates comes from without and subtly seeks to destroy democracy from within. It reminds one of the scriptural saying: "There shall arise . . . false prophets, and shall show great signs and wonders; so as to lead astray, if possible, even the elect." Indeed these new false prophets specialize in falsehood, knowing it is false, deceiving men by offering what they brazenly call a new and better kind of democracy. One obligation they never accept is the obligation to truth. It matters nothing to these prophets that the system they proclaim repudiates and contradicts everything that democratic man has striven and fought for through the ages, from the first dawn when the people began to resist the tyranny of unmitigated power.

Of all the attempts to identify liberty and democracy with their precise opposites none has been so vigorous or so blatant as that undertaken by Soviet communism, and none has been so potent or so dangerous. Only the most full-blooded Nazi could have been receptive to the Hitlerian nonsense about "German democracy" and its gift of "true liberty." But not a few have been deluded into believing that the Soviet system set up a new and better brand of democracy, or at least that if it rejected democracy as *we* now know it, it provided the foundation on which in time a new and greater democracy could be built. It did so by destroying the exploitative power of wealth, by rejecting all differences of class between man and man, and by abolishing all discrimination between group and group, between race and race. Those who accept this rosy view, in their laudable sympathy for exploited groups and for those who suffer from insecurity or discrimination in our very imperfect democracies, forget that the unbridled power of the few is more oppressive than inequalities of wealth and that wherever such power obtains it creates more deadly inequalities than those it claims to remove—in truth that the equality it offers to men and groups is in the end nothing but equality in servitude and degradation. They forget that totalitarian power by its very nature must clamp down all the creative impulses of a society and that it permits no way of deliverance save through the convulsions of the same violence from which it sprang. They forget that, however inadequate a democracy may be, it still maintains the open road along which men advance peaceably from equal rights toward equal opportunities.

Communist propagandists have sedulously proclaimed the democratic merits of their system. With Stalin they point to the Soviet Constitution of 1936 as the most democratic the world has known. They call their system the people's republic, the people's democracy, the state of the workers and peasants. They exhibit their elaborate apparatus of elections, in the local soviets, the regional soviets, and all the way up to the Supreme Soviet of the Union. So Stalin is "elected" by a vote one hundred per cent unanimous. So the candidates favored by the Party win invariably by a vote in their favor that only a certain arithmetical modesty reduces below the unanimity accorded to the All-Highest. So the voters are sometimes given two tickets, one with the name of the accredited Party member and the other blank, and asked, under the eye of watchful officials, to cast one or the other into the ballot box! Yet this travesty of the suffrage has been used by apologists like the Webbs to support the thesis that there is a working democracy in Soviet Russia. Of course the mere fact of elections is no criterion of democracy. There are elections, for example, in certain Latin-American countries but they do little to mitigate the rule of the *caudillo* and his clique—though in these countries, as not in Soviet Russia, there may be a real opposition party for which to vote. Wherever opinion is curbed, wherever propaganda is monopolized, wherever government can manipulate elections, wherever a considerable portion of the people either are not allowed to vote at all or are prevented by the fear of consequences from voting as they would, the mere writing of names on a ballot is an empty tribute to the ghost of democracy.

The test is simple. Can men freely and fully disagree with the policies of their government and still remain as secure as before? Can they freely organize in favor of policies contrary to those of their government? Can they freely vote against their government? Can they vote their government out of power when there is a majority or plurality of votes against it? Is there a constitutional requirement that elections to decide this issue shall be held at stated times or under stated conditions? If the answer is "no" to any of these questions the system of government is not a democracy. If the answer is not "yes" to them all we are confronted with some other kind of rule than that which from the first has been associated with the name of "democracy," as it has developed from the time of the city-states that first bestowed the name, as it has emerged in the age-long opposition to the tyrannies and the corruptions of irresponsible power.

From the beginning Marxist communism, even when it most sincerely attacked the economic exploitation of the workers, has been inherently anti-democratic. Karl Marx himself showed no interest in or appreciation of democracy. He had no belief in the will of the people, nor even in the will of the proletariat. "We are not concerned," he declared, "with what even the proletariat as a whole may regard as its aim." Historical necessity was superior to any such consensus of the ignorant, and the leaders who have seen the Marxist light, the chosen disciples, the "vanguard" as it came to be called by Lenin, will tell the people where they must go. Marx never even dreamed of a future democracy but only of a future "classless society," a kind of happy anarchy at the far end of the "dictatorship." Marx, the divider, the man of bitter hates, the impatient dogmatist, the brilliant propagandist of the revolution that would crush to earth all the things he loathed, Marx was not the kind of man who could have any sympathy for or understanding of the healing processes of democracy. Marx, like the rest of us, was "human, all too human." The iron had entered his soul. His philosophy was the vehicle of his emotions and his needs. Inevitably it was alien to democracy.

There came, however, the stage where Marxism succeeded in attaining power. Political expediency has led the inheritors of that power to assert with unblushing vehemence that they, and they alone, are the champions of democracy, that their system, and their system alone, is the embodiment of democracy. They call their states the "people's democracies," though the people have no control whatever over their affairs. Lenin set the example, and it was followed by Stalin, who declared that the Soviet Constitution of 1936 was the most democratic the world had known. Indeed it had a democratic ring, if you forget about the Party. Indeed it declared that all political power belonged to the working people —they are allowed to vote for their masters. But if any Russian worker should dare to assert that the Soviet State is not a democracy he would speedily receive a rather elementary lesson in the realities of power.

Today there is a great corps of propagandists who expatiate on the unique virtues of Soviet democracy. Here, for example, are the words of one of them, Andrei Y. Vishinsky, who first rose to fame as prosecutor in the famous "purge" trials. "The Soviet system of representation, the only democratic system in the world, expresses the indissoluble and complete authority of the Soviet people." But let us hear the argument at more length. Mr. Vishinsky cites the following passage from Lenin:

> The Soviets are the spontaneous organization of the toiling and exploited masses themselves, *facilitating* the possibility of themselves eliminating the state and governing it in every possible way. It is precisely the vanguard of toilers and exploited, the city prole-

tariat, which has the advantage that it is best united by big under-takings—it is entirely easy for it to elect and to follow up elections. Automatically the Soviet organization *facilitates* the union of all the toilers and exploited around their vanguard—the proletariat. The old bourgeois apparatus—officialdom, the privilege of wealth, bour-geois education, connections and so on . . . all this disappears under the Soviet organization. Freedom of the press ceases to be hypocrisy because the printing presses and paper are taken away from the bourgeoisie. The same occurs with the better buildings, the palaces, the private dwellings, and the landowners' houses. The Soviet authority took thousands and thousands of these better build-ings from the exploiters straight away, and thus made a million times more democratic the right of masses to assemble—the right of assembly without which democracy is a delusion.

Vishinsky then proceeds to the triumphant conclusion: "This is why Soviet democracy and the Soviet state are a million times more democratic than the most democratic bourgeois republic."

We observe in passing that Soviet propagandists don't ever argue with you. They try to smother you with assertions. They never offer the pros and cons. They never allow any counter-argu-ments to be raised. They use their "pros" as a bludgeon to destroy the "cons." There is not one statement in the above passage from Lenin that is not, beginning with the reference to "spontaneous organization," either dubious or flagrantly misused to convey a false impression, the false impression that a tyranny which em-ploys the language of democracy is therefore somehow trans-formed into his own opposite, that is, democracy.

We are not concerned with the Soviet system as it exists inside Russia nor with the misrepresentations of it that Soviet propagan-dists purvey to their own people. Our business is solely with the insidious effects of this propaganda when it is introduced into democratic countries by those whom it has convinced and still more by those who use it as a technique for the attainment of power. There it threatens our democracy in two quite opposite ways.

On the one hand it breeds confusion in the thoughts of a significant number of liberal-minded persons. The propaganda is insistent and skilful and utterly without scruple. It represents communism as an evangel of peace on earth, goodwill among men, coming to the rescue of the "exploited" everywhere, destined to overthrow the evil destructive forces of capitalism, imperialism, fascism, all of which are nursed by a monstrosity called "bourgeois democracy." It fastens on the weaknesses of democratic practice, the failures of democracies to live up to their ideals. It pillories, for example, the prejudice and discrimination that dishonor our democracy and paints in glowing contrast the equality and harmony that reign under communism. It exposes the economic insecurity of the workers under capitalism as against their complete security in the Soviet Union. Thus it appeals to our more naive idealists, to men and women whose hearts are in the right place but who are woefully ignorant of political realities. It makes a yet stronger appeal to members of those groups which have been betrayed by our democracies, which have been treated as inferior, unacceptable, second-class, or outcast. We cannot be surprised if some Negro leaders fall under the communist spell. We should not be surprised if some Jewish intellectuals are won over. We are to blame, not they. If we blame them we should blame ourselves instead. Besides these again, there are the disoriented, those who have been affected by the anomy of our times. Finally, there are seekers after power, ambitious unquiet men who find no other avenues open to their masterful desires. All these alike, from whatever impulse, spurred by whatever motivations, claim to be advanced liberals, the advocates of true democracy. Many of them are not actually communists but instead are unduly sensitive to its claims and unduly insensitive to its actual works. They all feel the urge of strong emotional drives. Thus by their vehemence and misguided enthusiasm they bring confusion into the councils of democracy. One aspect of this confusion we have already commented on—the use of the utterly misleading phrase "economic democracy."

Much attention has been called to the propagandistic success of Sovietism in winning over to its side or at least to a position of indulgent sympathy the various groups to which we have just referred. But the other aspect of communist encroachment on democracy, the more insidious aspect, has been largely disregarded. We must therefore give it fuller consideration.

———•—•———

Chapter Twelve

THE PERIL OF ANTIPATHETIC CONTAGION

While communist propaganda confuses and tends to divide the more liberal groups it has a very different but no less dangerous influence on the more conservative groups. It is an old observation that extremes breed counter-extremes, that intolerance prompts to a counter-intolerance, that the spirit of violence on one side generates a spirit of violence on the other. Recent history shows us how fascism has been evoked in countries where communism grew strong, winning more adherents the more formidable communism became. Mussolini would never have come to power had it not been for the communist uprisings in Northern Italy. It is highly probable that, had it not been for the quick growth of the communist party in Germany, Hitler would never have been given his fatal chance to ruin the German people. The communists and the anarchists of Spain—anarchism being only communism in reverse —confounded the young republic and prepared the way for the fascist dictator. But even where communists are a small minority without any chance of attaining direct power, as in the United States, their influence on the more timorous, on the less enlightened, and on the more conservative-minded is anti-democratic. The ways of communistic propaganda, here subtle and insinuating, there loud and aggressive, peculiarly tempt those who resist them to resort to methods of defense that dangerously approach the fascist mode. The revolutionary aims of communism become

THE PERIL OF ANTIPATHETIC CONTAGION

the justification for suppressive activities that resemble, if in a much milder way, the violation of civil rights characteristic of the communist's treatment of non-communists.

In some essential respects we keep the record clean. There could, for example, be no greater contrast than the Mindszenty trial in Hungary and the trial in New York City at the same time of eleven communists on conspiracy charges. In our courts pallid broken political prisoners do not make confessions that betray the loyalties that gave meaning to their lives, while we vainly seek to penetrate the dreadful secrecy of the treatment to which these prisoners were subjected. In our courts the judges are not the pup- pets of the government. In this particular case the eleven defend- ents had every possible legal aid and in the first instance were themselves allowed to bring charges against the impartiality of the jury system, against the competence of the court, against the judge. Their lawyers and they themselves indulged in an endless series of vociferous and disorderly protests, which were most patiently investigated by the presiding judge. Emphatically, so far as our major courts are concerned, we maintain toward com- munists those fair-minded democratic procedures that the com- munists so flagrantly deny to non-communists.

But in other respects, by a kind of unsympathetic contagion, we let our fear of communism lead us into an imitation of their ways. It is, for example, a favorite technique of communists to denounce as fascists all those who disagree with them. Some among us are doing the same thing in reverse. They label as communists all those who stand anywhere left of themselves, even when these others stand only a little left of center. They do not realize that in making such charges they are not only imitating the communist pattern but are undermining the democracy they profess to defend. The betrayal of democracy becomes yet more serious when these misguided defenders of a faith they do not un- derstand are dealing with radicals of any kind, with critics of the established order, socialists who may themselves be anti-com- munists, with those who have any sympathies for communism, and of course with communists themselves. All such groups are lumped together indiscriminately as "reds," and are denied the rights and immunities inherent in the democratic process. The House Committee on Un-American Activities has shown a lamentably undemocratic attitude in its treatment of certain witnesses before it. Our colleges and universities, while they have made on the whole a creditable showing, in certain instances have set a poor example. Some of them have been very zealous in barring student groups from inviting radical speakers. One college dismissed a professor whose immediate offense was that he had presided at a Henry Wallace meeting. A few colleges have resorted to autocratic methods in dismissing communists and persons suspected of communism. Municipal authorities in some states have denied the use of public halls to Wallace propagandists and other speakers who came under this category of "subversive" persons. Some states make it compulsory on teachers to take loyalty oaths, which suggests that they believe the undemocratic method of compulsion is more effective than the democratic appeal to reason. Bills now pending in certain states would make it a crime for school boards and colleges to employ communists.

Now there is no obligation on the part of any school or college to employ communists. And it is not unreasonable that educational authorities should include, in the information they require concerning candidates for positions, the question whether they are communists. This is not unreasonable, in the first instance because communists are committed to doctrines and to loyalties that may not unreasonably be regarded by these authorities as impediments to the open-minded pursuit of knowledge, at least in certain fields. It is, however, an entirely different thing to dismiss teachers from office because they are communists or merely because they have shown some leanings in that direction—unless there is definite evidence that they have used the classroom to propagate their politics.

It is an unwise thing to do on several counts. Dismissal is something entirely different from the balance of considerations that, as between competing candidates, may determine an initial appointment. The communist or near-communist is dismissed because it is claimed that he is not intellectually free. But where is it possible to draw a line? All men have their codes and their respective creeds of some sort. May not any such creed be regarded as prepossessing the holder to interpret evidences favorable to it? If you dismiss a teacher because of his beliefs and on no other ground you create the uneasy feeling that you in turn are making authority the arbiter of truth. And you give the communist in turn the argument that democracy exhibits the same intolerance of contrary opinion that it charges against communism. You are forgetting the acute reasoning of Mill's *Essay on Liberty* to the effect that even truth loses its virtue, as truth, when it uses coercion to suppress error. You are not showing the necessary democratic faith that the truth must prove itself in the free commerce of opinions. Freedom becomes a sensitive plant, ready to close at a touch, when authority becomes its guardian. One college ex-president well expressed the danger when he said: "I do not fear the influence of any extreme opinions in the academic world so much as I fear the attempt to stifle them and limit freedom of debate."

A peculiar risk of the resort to authority is that there are no frontier lines to mark the transgression on the liberty of opinion. If you dismiss communists from academic positions then you are most inclined to dismiss near-communists, fellow-travellers, radicals. They can all be embraced as coming under the convenient category of being "subversive." The term "subversive" has been used all too loosely by the Committee on Un-American Activities, and the term "Un-American" itself is all too loose a designation to be admitted into the title of an investigating committee. For the unreformed Committee anyone became in effect "un-American" if at any time he had been a member of an organization in which communists had participated. There are some college authorities who are similarly inclined, who regard any radical or socialist as being "subversive," and who are always looking for an opportunity to get rid of any such person. An example of how far the contagion can spread was exhibited at Oregon State College, where a scientist was dismissed because he adhered to the biological theory now officially endorsed in the Soviet Union, the theory of which Lysenko has in that country become the accredited champion. The President of that college justified his action, according to the report in *The New York Times,** as follows: "Any scientist who has such poor power of discrimination as to choose Lysenko's genetics against all the weight of evidence is not much of a scientist or has lost the freedom that an instructor should possess." It is hard to imagine a worse argument or one more detrimental to free scientific inquiry. The theory in question, the environmentalist theory of genetics, is of course not Lysenko's. It is one that has been held by quite reputable biologists. It is by no means *certain* that it contains no element of truth. The fact that the majority of biologists reject it is not conclusive. The majority of scientists in any particular field have sometimes been mistaken. But that is not the major issue here. Here we have the case of a college President who in his reaction against the intellectual tyranny of communism is led to take a course of action that not only defeats its own ends but gives the communists another opportunity to proclaim the insincerity of our democratic pretensions.

One of the commonest signs of unsympathetic contagion has been the increasing tendency on the part of school boards, municipal councils, and colleges to refuse the use of public halls or the forums of educational institutions to individuals or groups on the suspicion that they are "reds." In certain areas of the United States there has always been an undemocratic highhandedness in the denial of such facilities, but recently the tendency has been shown by authorities of whom better things might have been expected. For example, in the same month (April) of the year 1949 both the Cambridge, Mass., School Committee and the University of California at Los Angeles denied Mr. Harold Laski the opportunity to deliver an address on premises under their respective control. Mr. Laski has taken a leading part in the British Labor Party's struggle against Communist influence. He is a distinguished speaker who has had a distinguished career. The present

* February 24th, 1949.

author happens to be in frequent disagreement with his views but agrees thoroughly with him on this point, that such attempts to prevent him from being heard by groups who want to hear him are a disgrace to a country that professes to be upholding the banner of democracy.

Again, if you oppose such methods as being contrary to the democratic principle you are certain to incur suspicion in some quarters of being yourself a "red." Thus does Soviet communism spread contagion to foul the nest of democracy, by the suspicions it engenders, by the fears it instils, by the loud charges it makes, by the masquerade it adopts, by the provocative techniques it follows. But after all we should not blame hostile doctrines for our own shortcomings. We the insecure, unfaithful, superficial, interest-blinded democrats are to blame. The communists know absolutely what they want, and they go all out to get it. We are uncertain of our goals and we don't care enough about them. We do not know our own faith, we do not appreciate its worth. We are, too many of us, half-believers. Thus are we half-unarmed. And thus we run the danger of defeat.

It is so natural for people to conclude that what they think is wrong should be on that account forbidden. It is so hard for them to learn the first lesson of democracy, that no doctrine should be suppressed merely because they strongly disapprove of it. They are unwilling to put trust in the truth. They are not content to reason, to expound, to exhort, and to convince. They summon the policeman to support their "truth." So we move down the darkening road that leads to the prison-house of dogma and technological terror. It was this road that Germany followed, and thereby brought incalculable woe upon mankind, the woe that still broods over us today. The forces of barbarism lie in wait wherever the liberty of the mind is impugned.

There is another way in which our fear of communism is doing serious hurt to the cause of democracy. It affects our international behavior. Suddenly we are called to take the status of a world power. We cannot evade it any more. It has become our manifest destiny; it is indeed the inevitable consequence of what we are, what we have achieved, what we possess. At this time the future course of world history depends on how we behave to other peoples, on our relations and dealings with our ex-enemies, our wartime allies, all the countries that war has devastated, all the vast populations of the Orient, now stirring in distracted insurgence as they break through an ancient bondage. All these peoples are exposed to the counter-claims of the protagonists of two utterly irreconcilable political faiths. The communists are wiser in their generation than we are. They know what these peoples need, what they seek. The communists promise all aid and comfort to these peoples. They are as adept at making promises as they are at breaking them.

Fortunately for us, their behavior so belies their promises that only the most simple-minded trust them any more. On the other hand they are very successful, especially throughout the Orient, in misrepresenting *our* policies as those of rapacious exploiters, plotting to keep other peoples in subjection and misery in order to swell our imperialistic profits. And here we are sadly lacking in the high art of true diplomacy. We do not put ourselves in the place of other peoples. We do not try to understand their hardships and their problems. This high art of true diplomacy is the only way to enduring success. Not only do we generally lack it but we are led by our fear of communism to commitments that alienate these peoples. We ally ourselves with the reactionary forces that seek to return the peoples to their former bondage. These reactionary forces are fighting a losing battle, and we too are losing the fight when we take their side. We have done so in China and to some extent in Korea. We have not been guiltless of similar behavior in Germany and elsewhere in Europe and the Near East.

I am not suggesting that we wrap ourselves in a mantle of idealistic purity and refuse to cooperate with governments that do not subscribe to the American Bill of Rights. Politics, it has been said, is a choice of the second-best. In other words, we have to deal with things as they are, with all their messiness, with all their confusions, with all the embroilments of the distribution of power.

Only a minority of the peoples of the earth enjoy the benefits of democracy. Democracy must grow from within and its growth is generally slow. It cannot be imposed. Meanwhile we have to deal as best we can with undemocratic as well as with democratic governments. But we should do so only on our terms, making sure that our aid is to be used for the benefit of the people or at least to save them from worse evils. And we should certainly not take sides with more reactionary groups against more liberal groups, even though the latter have socialistic leanings. We ought to know by this time that European socialism is a quite different thing from communism and is no more welcome to the communists than American capitalism. In this matter, too, our fear of communism leads us into serious mistakes, mistakes that directly and indirectly do injury to the democratic cause.

We have so far been speaking of the dangers to the democratic cause that arise from the activities of communism whether in our midst or abroad. You will observe that the dangers we have reviewed are due not to the presence of communism, but to the fear of communism. This fear of communism turns out to be nothing else than the distrust of democracy. In the struggle against aggressive communist propaganda we are afraid, many of us, to maintain the ways of democracy. To their bold affirmation of their cause we present a timid negation of our own. That is the strategy of defeat.

What we must do is to recapture and to reassert the spirit of democracy, to make it ours, to make it live for our times and for our needs. If only we could realize what democracy means today, what the alternatives to it mean, what fateful decisions depend on our understanding of it and on our loyalty to it, we would exchange our fears for a victorious courage, vindicating our heritage to the inestimable advantage of all mankind. To this theme we finally turn.

Chapter Thirteen

THE TRUE ANSWER

Man is a social animal. He must belong, and have the sense of belonging, with his fellows. He must, in other words, share with them some social faith. He must, in a spiritual sense, speak the same language they speak, though he use it in his own way. In the last resort it is this social faith, and this faith alone, that unites him to his people. He must be the member of a great consensus. It is not enough that he join with other men in a common way of living, that he and they have various usages in common. Such things reinforce the consensus, they do not make it. It does not make the unity of a people that they have the same economic system and together possess the same storehouse of economic resources. It is not enough that they together form a common power or that they have at their command the great apparatus of a mechanical civilization. No resources, no machinery, no power can be a substitute for a binding faith. Without it a people is only a name, an aggregation, a statistical population, a geographical expression, a portion of the map.

Ever since man has been man his existence has centered about a social faith. It animated the primitive horde, the simple tribe, the members of the kin. What passed for religion was socially created. The Gods were the Gods of the people. Religion was a social faith before it became the more transcendent or universal faith we now call religion. The matrix of religion is the solidarity of the folk. And we may conjecture that even the more universal religions would not have developed were it not for the dawning of the larger "consciousness of kind." Religion could hardly have arrived at the concept of the fatherhood of God were it not for the vision of the brotherhood of man.

In olden days each folk had its own religion, and even in more advanced civilization the members of every community for the most part shared the same religious faith, accepted the same cultural values. That is true no longer, anywhere within the effective range of Western civilization. The old unity is lost and cannot be recalled. It cannot be restored unless we first abolish the specialization of functions in modern society, the flow of communications, the freedom of thought, the disturbing impacts of scientific inquiry, the liberty of men to form associations, according to the diversity of their interests and of their beliefs. Modern society must seek its solidarity along another road.

A modern people needs solidarity no less than did the peoples of a simpler world. And to have solidarity it must also have a faith, a system of values and standards to which it is committed. Without this social faith it cannot have even a fundamental law, for such a law is itself the reflection or part-expression of a faith. But this faith cannot be the all-inclusive faith of a simple people. It cannot be a religion, in the proper sense of that word. It cannot be an authoritative faith, the priests of which interpret its doctrines to the faithful. It cannot be a faith that provides an answer to the riddles of life. Such faiths, such philosophies, such theologies men must seek and find as members of other groups, no longer as citizens. The more intimate fellowships, the more particular worships, the more specific cultural devotions must find their focus elsewhere. The diversity of beliefs and modes of thought and cultural affinities prevent their unification under the aegis of the state.

Where then is to be found the unity of a people, of a nation, of the great multigroup countries of the modern world? Without unity the people falls apart, and the world itself can find no unity except on the basis of the unity of peoples. A people must feel its oneness. A people cannot find its oneness in the quest for bread, the quest for wealth, the quest for power; nor in the restless satisfaction of restless appetites. These things sustain no common good, no common will. These things, unless they are overruled by the deeper perceptions of the common good, divide and dissipate the community.

In this modern world there is only one faith that can sustain the unity of a people, the greater unity that gives free play to the richness of difference that makes the creative life of a community—and that is the faith of democracy. No other faith remains that can unite men as citizens, as members of the nation community. Every attempt to base the great community on any other faith means a resort to coercion, a rejection of the freedom of the mind, an intrusion of sheer force into the citadel of human personality, a barbarous invasion of the realm of values. Every attempt to unite men on any other basis, even if it is backed by all the engines of monopolized propaganda, means a tyranny not only over minorities who dissent from the faith but over the whole people. All totalitarian states set up a compulsory civil faith that inevitably grows more rigid, more iron-clad, more inhuman, until the faith itself becomes nothing but a disguise of the ideology of power.

Here then is the beauty of democracy, the exceeding fitness of democracy to meet the need of our complex multigroup civilization. The power of this faith is that it does not depend on power, but on a consensus that leaves other faiths free and still provides a ground on which the diversities of faith can stand. Thus in a genuine democracy men can belong to the solidarity of the whole and enjoy at the same time the spiritual sustainment of their particular faith and fellowship.

But here too is the peril of democracy. Since it admits all faiths it is easily conceived as being itself a purely negative thing, a form without content, a mere bracket to enclose diversity, a bloodless system for letting men and things alone in a neutrality of disinterestedness. Since it does not stand for the faith of any particular group it seems to stand for none of its own. But no union can be built on negatives. Democracy has a faith, a very positive and vital one. Our democracy, unhappily, has been slow to discover it and has done practically nothing to inculcate it. Thus we lack adequate defense against the robust insistent claims of other political faiths. We defend our own by a kind of groping instinct. Our counterpropaganda is often thin and weak, because it is couched too much in negatives.

In our times, when the clash of two political faiths holds the center of the world stage, when the response men give, all over the earth, to their respective claims becomes the voice of destiny, it is essential that we realize the positive meaning of the democratic creed. We must do so not only in order to meet, and robustly to counterattack, the wily propaganda of those who wish us ill, but even more in order to give resurgent life to our own cause and our internal unity. The worst disease of democracy is spiritual flabbiness, the lax contentment with negatives, the complacency that regards its freedom as purposeless vacancy within which each may go his way without obligation to the whole. When that attitude develops the disintegrating tendencies on which we have already dwelt take over and the cause is lost.

The first article of the democratic creed is the belief in humanity. Democracy puts its trust in the people. It holds that they should have the final right to determine their own affairs. It holds that they should be free to learn all the facts, to hear all views, and to decide accordingly. It holds that they should be provided with all the equipment and all the means necessary for the enjoyment of freedom. It holds that where the people have this right and these opportunities they will live a far richer and fuller life than when they are subject to the irresponsible will of any overlords. Thus the community of men can reveal its character and its potentialities, whereas under the authoritarian system the community is forever stunted and suppressed by the brutal power-intoxicated will of government.

This democratic trust in humanity is a faith in the capacities of the human being, as he is given the opportunity and the equipment to realize himself. It is a belief in the worth of the human personality. It finds here the key to all values. Unless the human person becomes a value for himself, unless he is invested with this dignity and this worth, unless even our ideas about God are intimately dependent on the sense of man's kinship with the divine, then all our search for values becomes vain or foolish. For man the only value that can have finality is the good life for man, the living and the enjoying of the good life—in the largest sense if you will, the pursuit of happiness. And the only way to that good life is the way of free experience, as men learn to relate themselves to one another and to the universal nature that embraces them. Democracy puts trust in the people—not in the masses, for "the masses" are a fluid collection of human beings who have lost or never possessed the integration of a people and thus can act only as a horde, driven this way or that by the blind impulse of passion or of need. Democracy alone creates a political people, making the goal of political endeavor the free evocation of the capacities of men within the social unity. The acceptance of this goal has essential positive implications, the positive tenets of the democratic faith. For example, it implies that free participation is more constructive than coercion. It implies that difference-breeding spontaneity is more desirable than uniformity-imposing coercion. It implies that the unity achieved through the integration of difference is more flexible, richer, more satisfying, more adventurous, more noble, than the unity achieved through the suppression of difference. It implies that a system that pulses with life in all its parts is finer and greater than one that is alive only at the all-disposing apex. It implies that the quality of living is more important than the manipulation of power.

The philosophy of democracy goes deeper. It aligns itself with the very principle of life. It is the miracle of life that it successfully refuses to be bound by the seeming mechanics of the physical universe. All other political systems ape the iron laws that govern the inanimate. But life creates, life generates, life synthesizes, life builds up its structure from within, life exhibits itself in endless variation, life succeeds by being different always from what it has been. Life does not abrogate one jot or tittle of the law that binds it to the inanimate cosmos; nevertheless it achieves what the inanimate forever lacks. Eternally it struggles for its own freedom and its own renewal. Eternally it combats chaos and uniformity and the lifeless clutch of power and the downward law of entropy.

So far as the great cosmos is concerned the hard distinction we here draw between the living and the inanimate may be no more than the way things appear to our ignorant eyes. Science has made astonishing advances in the knowledge of the physical universe but it knows completely nothing concerning the creative forces within it. It knows how the universe runs down, but it does not know how the universe builds up. Nor does it know how life builds up its countless forms. But for our purpose here the distinction serves as an analogy. It is sufficient that democracy, in its way, is true to the principle of life, in that it renews itself from within, in that it respects and utilizes difference and shuns uniformity, in that it animates the integral being of the body politic. Democracy lives in and through the community; dictatorship operates on the community from without, forever curbing its vital energies.

Here we see another aspect of the democratic faith. Under democracy, whatever else government may control or curb, it must respect the integrity of the culture that is born with the community and that blossoms into the myriad forms of art and style and taste and mode of living. Yet, as it grows and ramifies and diversifies and divides, it still remains one inclusive culture, the expressive tradition of the greater folk. All history is at depth the process of the making and remaking of such cultures, each of them a unique manifestation of the same humanity. Too often government has played havoc with human culture, clamping it with rivets of dogma or dragging it in the dust behind the chariot of power. No authoritarian state can allow men to seek the truth, wherever it may be found. It is the worst side of the evil genius of authoritarianism that in its fear and folly it must mutilate the nature of man, the expressiveness of the human spirit. It is the final glory of democracy that it not only suffers the spirit of man to reveal itself in freedom but also provides the positive conditions to encourage its free growth.

The democratic faith cannot be imposed on the peoples, as can the authoritarian faiths. It must instead be won by them. It must be maintained by their incessant vigilance. Thus it is a more difficult faith, for it puts a greater responsibility on the believer. It is not a faith for the inert, or for the socially uneducated. It is resented by the power-seeker, it is not congenial to narrow self-interest. It is scorned by the supercilious and the sophisticate, who do not understand the difference between the common and the vulgar, who do not perceive that while the vulgar is the shallowest, the common is the deepest thing in man.

"Democracy," said Carl Becker, is "a stupendous gamble for the highest stakes." Perhaps it is, but the risks of the gamble would be small if men could be taught to realize the value of what is at stake. Perhaps it is a gamble, but after all, in this realm of government, it is the only gamble men can win. Other systems of government may equally be thought of as a gamble, except that the people can never win. Marxism, for example, is a tremendous gamble for the Marxist but if he wins the people lose. The Marxist promises them a new freedom if he wins and if he does he imposes on them instead a new servitude.

Where the people know what the stakes are democracy can hardly lose. Its faith is so universal, so clear, so deeply rooted in human necessities and in human aspirations. Democracy loses only when it is not in earnest, when it betrays itself. Only the inertness of democracy, faced with the aggressive drive of its enemies within and without, can destroy it. Inertia is its death— the death of the people as community, under the barren rule of the men of power. As we have sought to show, our democracy is exposed to various perils, but all these perils, serious as they are, arise solely from the unreadiness of democratic countries—and not least our own—their unreadiness to understand democracy and to be true to its faith.

If then democracy is innately so superior, so much more rewarding, than the antidemocratic order that today competes so strongly, and so unscrupulously, for the allegiance of mankind, why is its victory, in the hearts of men, still so far from being assured? Does it not seem strange that in various countries large and determined groups still choose instead the rigid compulsions of dictatorial communism?

We have in the first place to remember that by far the greater part of the earth has had no experience of democracy. Nowhere in Asia or in Eastern Europe or in vast areas of Africa has democracy had opportunity to develop. In these lands the only contact most peoples have had with democratic countries has been of a peculiarly damaging kind. The Western powers exploited them, treated them as inferiors, subjected them. The liberties enjoyed by democratic countries were not regarded as articles of export.

The age of Western imperialism is past, but the memory and the consequences endure. The change of attitude shown in the American liberation of the Philippines or the renunciation at length of British imperialism in India came too late. All over the Orient there has spread a strong sense of nationality, and in its first stage it has been directed largely against the lapsing domination of the Western powers as well as against the complacent superiority long displayed by Westerners toward the colored races. Here Soviet communism seizes its opportunity. It proclaims itself the pure champion of the oppressed. It paints the blackest picture of the Western democracies as rapacious pirates. It identifies itself with the cause of revolution anywhere against the exploiters. It sends its agents in to instil the Marxist doctrine of revolution and thus to win these peoples to its side. It announces that imperialism is the last refuge of decadent capitalism and summons the peoples to join it in the victory of justice and liberty. And the peoples to whom it makes appeal have little reckoning of the prostration and persecution by means of which it rules or of the new imperialism it has itself extended over Manchuria and over the satellite countries of Eastern Europe.

We can then understand why in countries long dominated by the Western powers the propaganda of Sovietism should be so potent. But the question remains: why should the issue be in doubt in countries that have had experience of democracy? Why should Soviet communism offer any threat whatever to established democracies? And even in countries that are in no danger whatever of a communist revolution—for it is true that countries where democracy has been long entrenched are the most resistant to its influence—why should there still be so much fear of its influence? Could peoples who have enjoyed civil and political liberties ever elect servitude instead?

Some of our fears are exaggerated and some of them are misdirected. There is danger nevertheless. It lies, as we have already shown, not so much in the strength of our spiritual adversary as in our own democratic weakness. And that is why our fears so often miss the mark. We think, for example, we can save ourselves from the communist danger by rooting it out from our midst, whereas our only and our absolutely sufficient salvation depends instead on our more faithful devotion to the democratic cause.

For therein lies the answer at once to our question and to our fears. Who are those in a well-established democracy who are most susceptible to the propaganda of Sovietism? Let us leave aside the margin of psychopathic misfits and misguided utopians— they by themselves are of no account. The real "subversives" come from two groups, both of them suffering from a fatal insecurity, both of them brought to this condition because they have been betrayed by our unwillingness to put our democracy into practice.

One group consists of those who are haunted by economic insecurity—it is not poverty as such, though it brings its own evils, but the constant threat of poverty to come, the uncertainty of employment, the fear of loss of status, the haunting prospect of the later years of life when earning power is lost, that make men receptive to any system which offers assurance against these things. The incessant changefulness of modern society, the endless unpredictable ups and downs of business activity, work on the minds of men in ways that those who are relatively protected against their worst consequences rarely comprehend. As Walter Lippmann put it in an early book, it is these things that "breed the poisons of self-government." Men must be assured of life before they respond to the claims of the "good life." Democracy means little to them unless it first gives them the guarantee of a decent future. It must, where it has not already done so, protect them, as it so easily can, against needless economic hazards. Those who, in the name of "free enterprise," resist this claim do not understand the modern alternatives. Without these provisions men grope blindly for a new assurance and their ears are open to the siren appeals of the enemies of democracy.

The other group is one to which we have already given particular attention, because it is from this group that communism draws its most fervent, devoted, and effective converts. The converts from other groups are merely baffled or disgruntled men. This group suffers a deeper frustration, and those who feel it most sharply become avenging furies to destroy the democracy that has denied to them what it promises to all. Democratic peoples bring this evil on themselves when they discriminate against any body of citizens, when they treat them prejudicially as inferiors, when in effect they limit democracy by distinctions of race or color, of ethnic or national origin, of religious or social creed. Thereby they doubly betray their democracy. Not only do they sin directly against its primary tenets but they strengthen its enemies without and breed its enemies within. No human folly is more wasteful, or more destructive, than the discrimination of group against group. None is more contrary to the spirit of democracy.

In fine, we must make the democratic faith a positive and vital thing. We need a new assertion of dynamic democracy. We need to explore its height and its depth. We need to bring its meaning to the people. We have all the resources in the world—of what avail are they if we do not use them to build a greater and deeper fellowship among ourselves? We need to make democracy the doctrine of this greater fellowship. If we have the wisdom and the courage to do this we shall have built the ramparts of democracy against which all the forces of all its enemies will beat in vain.

NOTES AND COMMENTS

Notes and Comments

———•—•———

CHAPTER ONE

PAGE

4. OUR FAILURE TO EXPLORE THE NATURE OF DE-
MOCRACY. As late as a generation ago there was extremely
little interest in political doctrine, of any kind, in the United
States. The awakening of interest was then shown by the appearance of a number of competent works, those of Sabine,
Willoughby and Rogers, Cook, Maxey, Merriam, Coker, and
others. But of books devoted to the interpretation of democracy
there have been very few, and one still looks in vain for any
studies that deal with it in any profound or searching way. The
need, however, is being recognized. The challenge of opposing
doctrines brings the lesson that the really essential knowledge
about government is not to be attained through information
concerning administrative procedures. The citizen should learn
something about these things, but there is another kind of
knowledge that gives vitality to them and is itself vital. Professor F. O. Wilcox, as Chairman of the Committee on Under-
graduate Instruction of the American Political Science Association, has well pointed out our neglect of the concept of
democracy, remarking that "it is infinitely more important for
a student to think about these questions than it is for him to
know the steps a bill must go through before it becomes a
Law" (*American Political Science Review,* June, 1947).

5–6. HOW WASHINGTON, D. C., MISREPRESENTS THE NA-
TION. The capital holds to the Southern way, the way of

segregation. This way is repudiated by the government. It is repudiated by the majority of those who live at any time in Washington, D.C., who, however, as government employees with often only a temporary residence, have little to do with the city's affairs.

Nevertheless the city clings with particular obstinacy to its anti-democratic code, and constantly does damage to the reputation and to the interests of the United States by offering a new headlined exhibit of its prejudice. The Washington D.A.R. refuses to let Marian Anderson sing in its sanctified hall. The Capitol Transit Company defies successfully the efforts of the Fair Employment Practice Committee to make it modify its discriminatory stand against Negroes. The only legitimate theater in the city abandons dramatic performances rather than accept the Equity ruling against segregation. The Washington branch of the organization of university women secedes when the national association opens its doors.

One wonders if there is any way of revealing to the social elite who control this city and who are so proud of their ancestral Americanism that they are doing far more harm to the cause of their country than is done, say, by a group of gangsters or criminals. The latter do grievous injury to a relatively few, the former do a most serious wrong to the whole nation. By the manifestation of their prejudice they are prejudicing the prestige and the influence of this country within the whole range of the non-White peoples who form the greater part of the earth's population. These peoples are now coming to their own, and our future becomes more and more dependent on our relations with them. There is an intensive effort being made by the great White power that unhappily has no use for us or for our form of government to win them to its side *against us*. Our Washington elite, apart from the harm it is doing to us at home, is in its benightedness giving aid to the designs of this power.

CHAPTER TWO

13–14. ON THE NOTION OF EQUALITY. It is curious how little has been done to clarify, and how much to confuse, the meaning, the bearing, and the application of the most common words in the political vocabulary. The word "equality" furnishes an excellent illustration.

In the political context equality is asserted as a right, as a demand, not as a fact. In other words it is a claim that existing inequalities be removed. But what kind of existing inequalities, and on what ground? There is inequality everywhere in human society. And to complicate the situation there are endless *differences*, differences of interest, differences of disposition, differences of taste, differences of outlook, that cannot be called inequalities. There are other differences, differences of intelligence, of strength, of health, of fortitude, of endurance, and so forth, that are properly named inequalities, but often it is hard to draw the line between inequalities and mere differences. And it is still more difficult to say how far inequalities of the kind just mentioned are themselves inherent in human nature and how far they are responsive to socially determined conditions.

What then, in this welter of differences and inequalities, is meant by the assertion of equality as a right? It must mean one or more of three things, one, that *equality of treatment* should be established for all citizens, perhaps for all men, two, that *equality of opportunity* should be thus provided, and three, that *equality of equipment* should somehow be instituted.

(1) *Equality of treatment* is in the strictest sense identity of treatment. But in some relations that would be ridiculous, in others obviously undesirable. Should the judge exact the same fine for the same offense from the beggar and from the millionaire? Should the tax-collector take the same amount of income tax from the two? Or even the same percentage of their income? But again there are relations in which equality of treatment is regarded as desirable, inequality as offensive. The police, for example, should not be allowed to bully people who

are poor or humble, nor should these be denied in the law-courts equality of consideration with the prosperous or influential. It is a common saying that there should not be one law for the rich and another for the poor. And whenever we speak of "human rights" we think of certain fundamental securities, immunities, and liberties that should be assured alike to all men.

When then should men be accorded equality of treatment, in the strict sense, and when different treatment? What is it we want here? To what principle do we appeal? Surely not to the dead mechanics of equality but to the living value of fairness, *equity.* Equity transcends and abrogates the monotonous arithmetic of equality. As Aristotle said in his *Ethics,* equity is like a "leaden rule" that can be molded to fit the actualities of a situation, whereas without it law is a rigid yardstick that can measure only flat uniform surfaces. Equity makes law flexible, rational, ethical. To treat men equitably we must often treat them differently, according to their situation and their need. The goal is not equality as such but the provision for all of the social conditions under which they can enjoy as much well-being as possible, thus fulfilling their own lives.

(2) Here we arrive at *equality of opportunity.* This kind of equality makes a more reasonable and less ambiguous claim on us than some others. In the first place it expresses a genuine ideal. That all men should be as free as possible to develop their capacities, that intrinsic merit should not be blocked by needless material obstacles or by social discrimination—here is a principle that has a strong and clear appeal. Moreover it is a principle that does not involve the mechanical cutting up of distributable goods into equal portions. Instead, it requires the provision of social facilities of many kinds, so that each may move according to his capacity toward the particular goal of his own choice.

(3) At the other extreme stands the last of our trio, *equality of equipment.* It is the most soulless and the most dangerous of all the claims made in the name of equality. For now the abstract notion of equality asserts itself as a right. Purely for its own sake it bids men divide all things equally. It offers no

explanation why unequal men should possess equal things. What is the goal? What is the benefit to society? It is a grossly materialistic principle, for it is utterly inapplicable not only to spiritual and intellectual goods but also to the most double-edged of all the possessions of men—power over other men. Indeed, the tragic irony of this blind faith in abstract equality is that to achieve its objective it would ruthlessly endow the engineers of its program with a deadly and all-embracing power before which all other inequalities shrink into insignificance.

We have given here only the most rudimentary analysis of a very complicated theme. But it may suffice to justify the argument of the text, that the confusion of equality with democracy is full of peril.

18. INDIVIDUALITY AND INDIVIDUALISM. Individualism is a doctrine, the doctrine that in its political aspect regards governmental regulation, beyond an absolute minimum, as undue interference with the natural and beneficial equilibrium of society. Individuality is a quality, that complex of attributes of the human being that makes him a distinctive self among and beside his fellowmen. The doctrine of individualism justified itself as safeguarding and promoting individuality. But it conceived individuals as though they grew up in a social vacuum, as though they were relatively independent of the social matrix in which they lived and from which they derived the many-sided sustenance of their individuality. In this respect individualism was profoundly in error, although historically it did fulfill an important function by protesting against cramping, misguided, or antiquated forms of social regulation. On this subject see the author's *The Web of Government,* Chap. 1 § 2.

CHAPTER THREE

27. THE FUNCTION OF A PEOPLE IN A DEMOCRACY. In no country has the delusion that the people actually govern, that is, directly decide the numerous specific issues of govern-

ment, been so prevalent as in the United States. The early views of Walter Lippmann cited in the text are typical of the ideas still entertained by some, while in former days they were much more widely accepted. They went along with programs for the introduction or extension of such devices as the referendum, the initiative, the "recall." They go back to a time when local issues were more dominant and when the relative insulation of local communities was still considerable.

Correspondingly, there has appeared in the United States a series of writers who have attacked democracy on the ground that the people are incompetent to carry on the business of government. The people are too chaotic, too unruly, too unschooled, too much the prey of their blind emotions to conduct the great and delicate affairs of state. (See David Spitz, *Patterns of Anti-Democratic Thought,* New York, 1949, Chap. 4 and *passim.*)

This argument, as we have shown, tilts at a phantom democracy, but there is a more plausible argument that expresses contempt or derision for public opinion as the final maker and judge of governments. What is public opinion, it asks; where shall we find it? One form of the argument reduces it to the masked voice of financial magnates who own the major organs of opinion and lead the public "by the nose." Another form breaks it up into the opposing contentions of pressure groups as they struggle to capture the inert remainder of the voters. The total inadequacy of these conceptions of the nature of public opinion can readily be learned by any one who cares to study the history of the party system. In the countries of Western Europe, for example, there was in the period from 1850 to the outbreak of the First World War a continuous leftward change of party alignment that brought about a continuous change in the character and the policy of government.

To understand the nature and function of public opinion we must not think of it, on the other hand, as merely the arithmetic difference between the number of individuals who vote "Aye" and the number who vote "Nay." Those who think this way do not realize what a community means and what living in a community does to people. It is easy in these days of assiduous polling to fall into this error. It is an error into which the poll-makers themselves have grievously fallen. In an election the result must obviously be registered by the simple method of counting votes as separate units. But public opinion is not formed by individuals thinking and acting in detachment from their fellows. There are trends and currents that move and swell underneath. There is contagion and response. There is a sense of direction to which many are sensitive. Often the sophisticated are less aware of it than are the run of men. Ideas take hold, goals are apprehended, no one knows how. There are deep movements that work through generations and there are surface movements that change from day to day. There is a body of opinion that coheres and cumulates. There are tides of opinion and countertides. Public opinion is an ever-changing *system* of responses to forces that are more profound and far more significant than the ephemeral appeals of propagandists and orators. At any moment it may be unstable; sometimes it is excitable and swayed by waves of emotion; but in the course of time it regains its balance and moves steadily along its course.

Hence there is much hazard for the poll-makers who claim to measure its direction by dipping their buckets in the great sea. Their small samples are already motionless. From these they cannot project the strength of the quiet deep currents that constantly revitalize the spirit of democracy.

For a trenchant criticism of the superficial view of the nature of public opinion that, so far, seems to have been accepted by the majority of the poll-makers and to determine their measuring techniques, see Lindsay Rogers, *The Pollsters* (New York, 1949).

CHAPTER FOUR

31. "CAPITALIST DEMOCRACY." The quotation from Mr. Laski is taken from his *Democracy in Crisis* (University of North Carolina Press, 1933). Observe that socialism of a non-revolutionary or non-Marxist type—for example, the type once

PAGE

promoted by Robert Owen or that sponsored today by, say, Norman Thomas or by the British Labor Party—can *logically* maintain the compatibility of socialism and democracy, whereas the Marxist type can not. The logic of Marxism is invincibly anti-democratic, and the slogans of democracy are used by it in a propagandist way, whether it be to decry the "sham democracy" of other systems or to assert the "true democracy" of its own. The ideal government system of Marx and Lenin was the Commune, which would be "a working body, not a parliamentary body, executive and legislative at the same time." This meant that the body in question would be autocratic, neither reflecting nor representing public opinion. And Lenin goes on to say, "Democracy is a *state* recognizing the subordination of the minority to the majority, i.e., an organization for the systematic use of *violence* by one class against the other" (*State and Revolution,* Chap. IV, italics as in original). Neither Marx nor Lenin could conceive of any *state* that was anything else than a power structure through which one part of the population systematically used violence to suppress the other.

See also note on Marxism and Democracy under Chapter Eleven.

CHAPTER FIVE

40. FORMS OF THE ARISTOCRATIC FALLACY. All anti-democratic doctrines, with the exception of Marxian communism— and perhaps even that doctrine is only an apparent exception— are based on some concept of an elite who by reason of their superiority over "the masses" have a right to rule without respect for the opinions of the inferior multitude. In other words, they all imply the principle of aristocracy. The student of political doctrines should therefore note that the aristocratic fallacy assumes a number of different forms.

Before we classify these forms let us give a summary statement of the fallacy that is implicit in them all. It contains at the same time a misconception of the problem of government and a misconception of the character of democracy. The first we may call the "utopian fallacy," the second the "government by the people" fallacy.

(a) *The utopian fallacy.* Take, for example, the words of one of our aristocratic critics of democracy. According to Alleyne Ireland (*Democracy and the Human Equation,* New York, 1921), the government of man should be carried on not by "numbers" but by "intelligence," by the qualified few and not by the unqualified many. Who then allocates government to the qualified few? Themselves? Or God? How do the men of power come to submit to their rule? How do the unqualified many, who *ex hypothesi* do not elect them—for that would be democracy—come to obey a superiority they cannot even recognize? And when by some miracle these eminent ones sit on their thrones, how do they escape the temptations, the rivalries, and the corruptions of uncontrolled power? The whole concept belongs to the politics of cloud-cuckoo land.

(b) *The "government by the people" fallacy.* This is the fallacy to which attention is given in the text. It assumes either that the people themselves rule and, being incompetent, rule incompetently or, when it is dislodged from this position, that the people, being incompetent, elect incompetents to rule them.

The aristocratic claim takes a variety of forms according to the nature or the source of the superiority accredited with the right to rule. We may distinguish the following types and subtypes.

Type One: *the aristocracy of the breed.* The generic presumption is that men are of different clay, that by nature some men are born to rule and some to be ruled.

(a) *The nobility versus the commonalty.* The old doctrine of aristocracy was a class doctrine of a simple sort. A small portion of the population possessed power and prestige and wealth. They constituted the noble families, the upper class. They were the "blue blood" of the community, the natural rulers. Nature was hierarchical. The right ordering of society depended on the maintenance of a system of rank or degree. To disturb it was to interfere with the order of nature itself. "Take but degree away, untune that string, and, hark, what discord follows!"

(b) *The superior race versus the lesser breeds.* The racialist doctrine has several varieties. It is the doctrine that justified slavery and it is still the doctrine that justifies the discrimination and the segregation to which the Negro and more generally the non-White are subjected in the United States and elsewhere. It is the doctrine that justified imperialism, as expounded, for example, by Rudyard Kipling. And it is the doctrine that has always been congenial to dominant peoples, that has found modern pseudo-scientific expression in the writings of de Gobineau and Lapouge, of Houston Stewart Chamberlain and Rosenberg, and that was fanatically carried into fatal practice by Adolf Hitler.

(c) *The superior versus the inferior stocks.* This is the modern Darwinian variety of the doctrine. Unlike the others it is a doctrine of social mobility. The superior stocks naturally rise to the top, the inferior descend, in any society that permits the free competitive struggle. Democracy, assert the advocates of the doctrine, clogs or arrests this beneficent process by catering to the incompetent, by sheltering them from the struggle for survival, by encouraging them to breed and by discouraging the higher stocks, and of course by conferring on the unfit the right to choose the government, so that with their larger numbers they win out over the biologically fit. This theory has had many proponents in the United States, among the more recent being Madison Grant, E. M. Sait, and N. J. Lennes.

Type Two: *the aristocracy of prior authority.* This is the claim that a particular group or the members of a particular organization are invested with an authority derived from the sanctity of their mission, office, or origin. In its pure form it is theocracy, in which the ruler is the vice-gerent of God. In a modified form it is the doctrine of the ecclesiastical hierarchy who command the allegiance of the secular ruler and make his legitimacy depend on the unction they bestow. The aristocracy of class, with the monarch at its head, has often sought to buttress its claims by invoking this doctrine also. The chiefs are the offspring of the Gods. Kings are by God appointed; they rule by "divine right." The powers that be are ordained of God.

Type Three: *the aristocracy of specific merit.* This doctrine overlaps some varieties of Type One, but it does not necessarily imply the biological or racial postulate. Its special feature is that it takes some particular kind of virtue or quality as entitling those who possess it to rule. The virtue thus enthroned may be conceived ethically, as some kind of "goodness." Or it may be construed intellectually, as cleverness, intelligence, practical wisdom. The aristocratic standard of Plato, when he wanted philosophers to be kings, combined in characteristic Greek fashion the two notions, the philosopher being the man of wisdom who therefore followed the way of "virtue." A more arid version of the same doctrine has been propagated by the American group of falsely self-styled "humanists," led by Irving Babbitt and Paul Elmer More, who deplore the substitution of democracy for the aristocratic governance of an ascetically-minded discipline-imposing elite of "character and intellect." Somewhat more graciously George Santayana yearned for the Platonic "timocracy," the government of the men of merit.

Another variety of the type holds simply that government belongs to the men who have the native drive to power, the strong adventurous spirits who are cramped by the democratic process, the men of action who are born to be leaders and are not the kind to submit to the verdict of the many-headed populace. This conception has been particularly favored by an Italian school of thought. For example, it found typical expression in the utterances of D'Annunzio and Mussolini. A not dissimilar idea is given an industrial setting by James Burnham (*The Managerial Revolution,* New York, 1941), though he holds that his "managers" inevitably control the reins of power, not so much that they are the people who *should* rule.

For a searching critique of modern American aristocratic philosophies see Spitz, *op. cit.*

The quotation from Irving Babbitt is taken from his *Democracy and Leadership* (Boston, 1924); that from Fulton J. Sheen is to be found in his *Freedom under God* (Milwaukee, 1940).

CHAPTER SIX

PAGE

50. THE DEFINITION OF DEMOCRACY. Many of the attempts to define democracy miss the mark. Moreover there is
often doubt as to whether some particular state at some particular time is properly to be named a democracy. Why then
should there be so much more difficulty about the definition of
democracy than about the definition of other forms of government?

One reason is that democracy is a system that historically has
grown out of oligarchy, passing through a series of stages. At
what point in the transition it becomes democracy is one of
those questions of the less and the more that can have no precise answer. Another reason is that democracy, in the strict
sense, can exist for a limited body of citizens and yet be denied
to a portion of the people. Thus there was full democracy at
Athens for the privileged citizen group, but outside it there
were many disfranchised residents and a large body of slaves.
Athens was a democracy, but a partial democracy, limited and
maimed by the refusal to extend the democratic principle to
many of its subjects, one class of whom were denied the most
elementary of liberties. Similarly a state can be a democracy
in its domestic structure while nevertheless it is an imperialist
dynasty so far as its colonies are concerned. Again, the United
States is a democracy but still fences off, by one evasion or
another, an area of Negro subjection. We may also include
among partial democracies those democratic states that deny
women the right to vote.

Observe, however, that there is a difference of kind, not
merely of degree, between *all* democratic states, however partial they may be, and oligarchies or dictatorships. In democratic
states there is a way of governing and being governed that is
absent in non-democratic states. In a dictatorship there is a
privileged group of citizens just as there was a privileged group
in Athens in its hour of democracy, but the democratic structure did exist in Athens and it does not at all exist in a dictator-

ship. There is a particular political structure that marks the presence or absence of democracy.

This structure may be characterized in various ways, so that a further reason for our confusion about the meaning of democracy is that different observers choose different aspects of this structure for purposes of definition. Thus the democratic structure differs from the non-democratic in the following ways:

(1) the determination of government by free majority-decision;

(2) the right of minorities to organize and to propagate their doctrines;

(3) the supremacy of the legislative function over the administrative and executive functions—the "rule of law;"

(4) the supremacy of constitutional law, whether written or unwritten, over the will of the government in power;

(5) the derivation of political *authority* solely from the mandate of the electorate;

(6) the constitutional recognition of the distinction between the community and the state, so that the government of the state is conceived of as the agent of the community as a whole;

(7) The existence of voluntary associations not subject, so far as their objectives are concerned, to the control of government and not co-ordinated into the political structure;

(8) the constitutional guarantee of the liberty of religion, philosophy, art, and science, and broadly of the whole realm of culture.

All these features—and others might be added—logically cohere into a unified system. At the same time they can all be logically derived from, just as they are all practically involved in, the primary characteristic of the democratic structure as given in the text.

51. DEMOCRACY AND THE LIBERATION OF THE MIND. In the longer history of mankind no contribution of democracy

is so important as its charter of liberty for the inquiring questioning mind. Democracy admits and fosters the always disturbing but always needed scrutiny of the "idols of the tribe." In the longer run every kind of polity depends on public opinion, on the acceptance by the people of the "myth" that is congenial to it. But all other kinds, to bulwark the congenial myth, discourage and repress the inquiring mind, enthroning the authority of the established regime. Thus free speculation is taboo.

Hence the great advances of creative thought have been made by the peoples who also prepared the way of democracy. Other people might excel in the decorative arts and the elaboration of techniques. But these worked for the most part within the bounds of their traditions and their established lores. As the Roman poet Lucretius triumphantly said (*De Rerum Natura,* Bk. I) it was first a Greek—or rather a remarkable company of Greeks—who broke the bounds of thought and dared to pass beyond. These Greeks lived in the little areas of Greek democracy during the short period while that first great experiment in democracy survived. And all later generations have remained in their debt. They taught the Romans, and when the mediaeval world woke from its intellectual dreaming and science and philosophy took new life it was under the stimulus of the Greek way of thought. So up to our own times, through the free cities that broke the bonds of feudalism, up through the Western peoples that created the science and the philosophy of the modern world, democracy and the liberation of the mind have gone hand in hand.

CHAPTER SEVEN

59. DEMOCRACY AND DISCONTENT. Democracy, of all forms of government, provides the most free vent for discontent; dictatorship, more than any other form, denies any vent whatever.

Democracy not only allows every form of discontent to manifest itself, to protest and to appeal, but also provides a constitutional medium for the channeling of opposition to the party in power. Since alone it has no fear of the people it welcomes this opposition and is in fact dependent on its free and full expression. Dictatorship on the other hand is obsessed by the fear of discontent. By driving it underground it magnifies its fear. It must resort to desperate measures, regardless of the fact that it thereby in course of time increases the pressure underneath.

We find here one reason for regarding a well-established democracy as potentially the most enduring kind of government. It accommodates itself more flexibly to the processes of inevitable change. It is directly responsive to changing needs and changing attitudes. Dictatorship is cramped by its own iron laws, by its obsession with power, by its remoteness from the community, and by its perennial fear.

62–63. DEMOCRACY AND CAPITALISM. The association of democracy and capitalism is in the first instance an historical one. Democracy developed with the rise of a middle class, and the middle class became greatly strengthened with the growth of industry and consequently of capital, which became mainly a middle-class acquisition. Under feudalism the middle class was too small and weak to challenge the ruling class. It was the power acquired by the middle class, particularly through their industrial achievements, that finally overthrew the close-knit monarchical absolutism that supervened on the decay of the feudal order.

The current antithesis between the socialist state and the capitalist state is, however, misleading. The true distinction is between socialist states in the full sense, that is, states which have nationalized the whole apparatus of production, and socio-capitalist states, that is, states which combine an area of collectivism with an area of private production and exchange. Every modern state, outside the communist system, is socio-capitalist, the "mixture" being everywhere different and always changing. The trend of socio-capitalist states has been toward a higher degree of collectivism. See the author's *The Web of Government*, pp. 461–462.

64-65. THE DETACHMENT OF MODERN MAN. The appeal of totalitarianism, that is, of the various forms of modern dictatorship, lies in the promise it makes of restoring the lost primitive unity in which man was one with his total society. This is alike the promise of Hegel and of Marx, but Hegel appealed to the sophisticated conservative whereas Marx appealed to the drifting radical. The impressiveness of both schools lies, in the judgment of this author, in the skilful way in which they dressed up and rationalized a primitive emotion that is still deep-rooted in modern man, the emotion that seeks a simple identification with the whole scheme of things. The fact that the *simple* identification is unattainable is sufficiently established by the inevitable resort of both schools to a system of utterly coercive controls designed to suppress or liquidate all the refractory elements in man and in society. A unity that makes the ruler a kind of God and keeps him so by aid of the secret police, a unity that destroys all the spontaneous impulses of creative culture, a unity, run by a small clique, that rejects all morality, and all religion but its own, that emasculates all the organizations of the free community, is factitious, false, and unenduring.

Democracy accepts the social reality and therefore abandons the quest for the restoration of the primitive unity. The unity of life becomes multiform and thus can be comprehended only by the inadequate insight of individual and group. But in turn it sustains all the values of living, bidding men find their unity as best they can. It purifies religion, no longer corrupted into an instrument of power. It liberates art, no longer debased into a weapon of the propagandist. It restores the community and makes the nation an unwalled member of the yet greater community struggling to be born, the community of man.

CHAPTER EIGHT

69-70. THE NEGRO IN THE UNITED STATES. For an authoritative all-round account of the situation of the Negro see E. Franklin Frazier, *The Negro in the United States* (New

York, 1949). For the problem as a whole see Gunnar Myrdal, *An American Dilemma* (New York, 1944). For the anti-discrimination movement see the author's *The More Perfect Union* (New York, 1948).

CHAPTER NINE

76. ROUSSEAU AND THE "GENERAL WILL." See his *Social Contract,* Bk. I, Chap. VII and Bk. II, Chaps. I–III.

77. "ANOMIE." The word "anomie" is found much earlier but was reintroduced and given its modern direction by Emile Durkheim. The most distinctive recent contribution to the subject is the study by Robert K. Merton, "Social Structure and Anomie," in Ruth Nanda Anshen (ed.), *The Family: Its Function and Destiny* (New York, 1948). The present author, however, does not accept Professor Merton's rather exclusive association of anomy with capitalistic competitiveness but views it as being more broadly responsive to (a) culture clash in modern society and accompanying it the discrimination of group against group and (b) the violence of change, especially when the mobility and insecurity of modern man turn into disorientation under conditions of war or crisis.

79–80. DEMOCRACY AS BALANCE OF GROUP INTERESTS. For the earlier balance theory see *The Federalist,* Nos. X, XLIX–LI. Here already there is present the notion that specific types of economic interest, agrarian, mercantile, manufacturing, financial, and so forth, divide the people into opposing classes each of which is "actuated by different sentiments and views." Little indication is given of inclusive or communal sentiments and views to mitigate the demarcation between each of these classes. It is a more modest form of the Marxist position that economic function not only determines social class but also involves a total opposition both of interest and of ideology between classes. In the Hamiltonian doctrine these classes are conceived to constitute a relatively non-hierarchical social structure. Broadly, the lines of demarcation do not lie horizontally across the pyramid of power (see the author's *Web of Government,* Chap. V, § 3) but vertically down through it. In the Marxist doctrine there is of course one all-determining horizontal line. The Hamiltonian scheme admits the possibility of democracy as an equilibrium of interests. Somehow government regulates them, keeps them in leash so that no one overpowers the rest. Not dissimilar is the position of modern writers such as Bentley. Pressure groups differ in power, but no one is potent enough wholly to dominate, so a compromise or "adjustment" is attained. We have however criticized in the text the idea that democracy can endure as a mechanical equilibrium of this sort. On the other hand the Marxist position negates the existence of democracy altogether—so long as any classes whatever exist. This viewpoint resembles in turn the doctrine of non-Marxist writers such as James Burnham in *The Managerial Revolution,* where his "managers" in effect constitute a ruling class.

The identification of an interest group with a social class and then the identification of a social class with a whole inclusive and exclusive system of attitudes, policies, and ideologies are unwarranted assumptions. No one doubts that economic interests ramify far and predispose to congenial attitudes and doctrines. But the theories in question impatiently simplify the truth. The fact of wider interests that transcend differences of function and status is revealed in many ways. Otherwise group anarchy would be universal in human society. Specific evidence against these false identifications is provided by modern sociological research. It brings out, for example, the manner in which political attitudes cross the lines of economic groups. It shows that a social class is not properly defined as an interest group, even though there is a cluster of economic interests particular to each social class. It shows that the thinking and feeling of human beings is in no way divisible into the thinking and feeling of compartmented groups. There is on the one hand a sense of the communal well-being that struggles with the dividing interests of opposing groups. There is on the other hand a great overlapping of attitudes and social viewpoints across the

PAGE

lines of economic stratification and social class. For fresh evidence on this subject see Richard Centers, *The Psychology of Social Classes* (Princeton University Press, 1949).

82. THE SLAUGHTERHOUSE CASES. What made the decision of the Supreme Court in the Slaughterhouse Cases (1873) so important was that it practically nullified the major purpose of the Fourteenth Amendment. This Amendment was directed to the protection of *individuals* against the infringement of their civil rights by the states. It had the Negroes of the Southern States particularly in mind, but it applied to all groups equally. For this purpose it imposed three limitations on state action. No state, it said, (1) shall "make or enforce any law which shall abridge the privileges and immunities of citizens," (2) shall deprive "any person of life, liberty, or property without due process of law," or (3) shall "deny to any person within its jurisdiction the equal protection of the laws." The Court so restricted the interpretation of these provisions as in effect to leave individuals no protection against state encroachment on civil liberties. The Supreme Court did not move from this position until around 1925, but since that date, and particularly since 1937, has handed down a series of decisions reinterpreting the "due process" clause so as to make it apply to the protection of fundamental personal rights and liberties against state encroachments. For a synopsis of recent cases see Morroe Berger, "The Supreme Court and Group Discrimination Since 1937," *Columbia Law Review* (February 1949, Vol. 49, 201–230).

CHAPTER TEN

85. DEMOCRACY AND ANOMY. We do not imply that the social detachment and the denudation of value-obligations we call anomy occurs only under democratic conditions. In various civilizations of the past it has at some stage characterized an upper or leisure class. For example, the picture of the Roman leisure class presented by Martial and Juvenal indicates a condi-

tion of anomy. Oswald Spengler in his pretentiously erudite *Decline of the West* takes the exaggerated view that every great civilization declines at length into a state in which all the bonds of community are loosed, a state of value dissipation, the final stage or "winter" of the civilization as a whole.

The student should notice that moral unscrupulousness, the disregard of the moral standards broadly approved in a society, does not connote anomy, provided the groups exhibiting this disregard have nevertheless a code of values of their own, a code which they hold to be binding on themselves and do not treat merely as a means to their individual interests.

The association of democracy with anomy is then a special one. It springs from the fact that whole peoples, such as modern nations, no longer share any one religious code—except perhaps nominally or as an historical but outworn tradition. Likewise within every modern community there are the divergent moral codes of different groups, not one all-prevailing code such as the customary law of simple peoples. The problem then is to find a bond of cohesiveness for the people as a whole. In the totalitarian state this is provided—so long as it endures—by the political religion that by ceaseless indoctrination and inquisition is imposed on the people. Democracy can have no such recourse, and unless it succeeds in inspiring a free system of congenial common values it will not hold a people together. The operation of centrifugal forces breaks it down and prepares the way for anomy.

89. COMMUNISM AS REFUGE FROM OR REVULSION FROM ANOMY. The reader should particularly observe that doctrines of a violent divisive type, such as communism, are not as such expressions of the anomic attitude. In a sense such doctrines are at the opposite pole from the anomic position. They are doctrines of a false solidarity, one engineered and maintained by violence and "liquidation." Since, however, the anomic person can no longer enter into a free solidarity, while yet he may find the state of social detachment an intolerable void, he may in his revulsion seek release and "redemption" by embracing the compulsive discipline of an imposed solidarity, such as communism offers him.

96. ELECTIONS UNDER THE SOVIET SYSTEM. Nothing witnesses more clearly to the wilful, though sometimes also naive, parody of democracy exhibited in communist countries than the "unanimity" or approach to "unanimity" shown in election returns for important offices. Such "unanimity" is the surest proof that democratic conditions are absent. Wherever opinion is free men divide on all current political issues and on the choice of leaders and representatives. Indeed it lies in the very nature of democracy that the questions to be determined by elections are controversial ones. The law of human nature, that public opinion plays out in a broad band from right to left, is not abrogated in the Soviet system. Even if we assumed that the communist ideology ruled in every Russian heart there would be no more unanimity on *policy* than before. Where you have the appearance of unanimity in election results it is an obvious sign of the application of coercion and the strong persuasion of fear. Apart from this aspect altogether, where only one party is allowed to exist, the resort to elections loses all democratic significance, for in a democracy the main function of elections is precisely the arbitrament between parties and their respective programs.

The word "unanimity" has become one of the major maskwords of the Soviet tyrants. So long as the appearance of unanimity is maintained, i.e., so long as their terror is potent enough to maintain it, they blandly call it the voice of the people, of the indivisible people. The same word "unanimity" is lavishly employed as a euphemism for the veto system they insist upon in all international councils. To modify an old story, they say in effect: "Gentlemen, there must be unanimity; we insist upon it."

97. MARXISM AND DEMOCRACY. Marxists do not discuss democracy. They merely take over the word in order to gloss over their own form of tyranny or dictatorship. Marx himself

never dealt with the question of democracy. He attacked the only form of democracy that has developed under modern conditions, the parliamentary form. His model of the future state, so long as a state should exist, was the Commune, and the Commune, he insisted, would have a centralized authority that would use the suffrage only as an employer might use it "in the search for the workers and managers in his business" (*The Civil War in France*). Lenin in turn gloated over the destruction of parliamentarianism and heralded the day when, as Engels had said, the new order would "throw on the scrap heap" democracy and every other kind of "state rubbish" (see Lenin, *State and Revolution,* Chap. *IV*). There was a spirit of violent intolerance in Marx and Lenin that could never have accommodated itself to the principles of democracy. Lenin fulminated against any suggestion of mitigating "the iron discipline of the Party"—an attitude that was unconditionally shared by Stalin (see Stalin, *Foundations of Leninism,* Chap. VIII).

97. MARX ON THE PROLETARIAT. The quotation comes from *The Holy Family.*

98. VISHINSKY ON DEMOCRACY. Mr. Vishinsky's book, *The Law of the Soviet State* (Eng. tr., New York, 1948), while professing to be a straightforward account of the Soviet legal and constitutional structure, is violently propagandistic throughout. The first quotation is taken from page 352 and the second from pages 42–43 of that work. The Lenin passage is given as from Lenin: *Works* (Russian ed.), Vol. XXXIII, p. 350.

CHAPTER TWELVE

105. The college ex-president referred to is Herbert Davis, formerly President of Smith College, as quoted in *The New York Times,* May 30th, 1949.

105. THE HOUSE COMMITTEE ON UN-AMERICAN ACTIVITIES. This committee, which has been in being since 1938 and

was made a standing committee in 1947, occupies a rather anomalous position. Its particular function is to propose to Congress, after due investigation, measures to combat "subversive" activities. Its main business, however, has been that of holding public hearings, to which it summons people suspected of "subversive" views, and of giving wide publicity to the resulting exposure. Its members are not, for the most part, particularly well qualified for the task they undertake. In some of them the judicial quality has been sadly to seek. These members do not seem to realize that charges publicly vented will damage a reputation even if the charges are at a later stage withdrawn or remain unsubstantiated. They have no defined standards of what they mean by "subversive" or "Un-American." They do not follow the rules of evidence that are accepted and applied by the courts of law. They have blacklisted public-spirited citizens who happen to be more "radical" than themselves or who at one time or another supported some movement that enlisted any communists on its side. In short, their procedures have too often lacked proper restraint, discretion, and dignity. It may indeed be questioned whether a committee of this type is a qualified watchdog of the national safety. After all, the F.B.I. is assumed to do this kind of investigation, and its members are assumed to have special training for their job. At the least it is under unified authority and does not conduct its investigations before the eyes of the public.

107–108. THE SUCCESS OF THE SOVIET'S CHARGES OF IMPERIALISM AGAINST THE WEST. By far the most rewarding to the communists of the endless propagandistic onslaughts they make against Western democracies has been the accusation of imperialism. Most of their other charges against the "exploiters" of the "toilers" now fall flat and convince only the converted. But the peoples to which they appeal against Western imperialism are predisposed to receptivity. They *have* been exploited, they *have* been treated as "lesser breeds" by the industrially advanced and more powerful peoples of the West. It is true that they have generally been oppressed as much and often more by their own feudal potentates and that the West has brought to them alike the technology and the training and the political doctrines that have made possible the great uprising. But here too Soviet propaganda has been more potent and more skilful than the counter-activities of the West. For the Western powers have favored the old regimes against which the new nationalism was revolting and thus have turned the leaders of the revolt to the side of communism. Thus the communists have won China and made great progress in Viet-Nam, in Indonesia, in Malaysia, in Burma, and in some areas even in India.

The modern Soviet doctrine of Western imperialism is Leninist, not Marxist. Lenin "discovered" that imperialism is the last refuge of decaying capitalism, the "highest stage," the stage in which it perishes (Lenin: *Imperialism, the Highest Stage of Capitalism*). Capitalism becomes now "monopoly capitalism." Capitalism was doomed by Marx because of its inevitable "contradictions," the falling rate of profits, the inability of the swollen "proletariat" to buy the goods produced by the ever smaller number of ever bigger capitalists. So it resorts to exporting to the rest of the world, which is divided up by the capitalist powers in a furious search for markets. The theory itself is full of economic fallacies but it had wonderful propagandistic advantages. It explained to the faithful why the prophecies of Marx about the early demise of capitalism were not fulfilled. It explained why the communist revolution occurred, not in an advanced capitalist society but in a belated feudalist society, that of Russia. Above all, it broadened the appeal of Marxism, which had been addressed essentially to industrial workers and not to peasants, so that it now included the industrially undeveloped peoples within its range. Stalin, for example, summed up the Leninist position as follows: "The world is divided into two camps: the camp of a handful of civilized nations, which possess finance capitalism and exploit the vast majority of the population of the globe; and the camp of the oppressed and exploited peoples in the colonies and dependent countries, who comprise that majority (Stalin: *Foundations of Leninism*, Chap. VI).

CHAPTER THIRTEEN

PAGE

110. RELIGION AND SOCIAL SOLIDARITY. It is noteworthy that those peoples who form an enclave in the midst of larger peoples or who feel for some other reason that their identity is threatened cling more tenaciously to their particular religious faiths and generally observe more faithfully the rituals of their religion. Religion becomes for them the refuge of an endangered solidarity. This has notably been the case, throughout the centuries, with the Jewish people. Out of numerous other instances we might cite those of the French Canadians and of the Irish.

114. THE CONCEPT OF THE MASSES. The expression, "the masses," is always a loaded one and always reflects an undemocratic theory of the social structure. In old literature it conveyed a sharp distinction between a relatively small cultured upper class and a lárge indiscriminate uncultivated lower class. This usage was still regular in America in the revolutionary period. The Marxists took over the expression as equivalent to the proletariat, still accepting the theory that society was divided into two clear-cut classes. In modern usage the singular form "the mass" is used not infrequently as referring to an aggregate of people, without a distinctive class connotation, as in "mass response," "mass persuasion," and so on. The plural form is found in a variant of the older usage, connoting a group or a people that has become detached from its social or psychological moorings to assume a kind of indiscriminate insurgence or domination. This phenomenon is, for example, the theme of Ortega y Gasset's *The Revolt of the Masses.*

115. DEMOCRACY AND CULTURE. At this stage of the argument it should be clear that the primary distinction between democracy and the other forms of government is the fact that under democracy culture is integrally free. Democracy alone, by constitutional principle, refrains from any direct or deliberate interference with the cultural processes that are the life of the community. Old-style oligarchies generally regulated culture in two

ways, first by curbing any cultural directions that seemed a threat to the established order and second by limiting and thus controlling the cultural development of the subject classes. Often, though not always, they also sponsored an official religion which became a strong buttress of their authority. Modern dictatorship, the totalitarian kind, goes much further and claims a total control over all cultural activity. Every aspect of human living becomes political and must be "co-ordinated." For a fuller discussion see the author's *The Web of Government,* Chap. VIII § 2 and Chap. XIII.

Why is it, we ask in passing, that the most inquisitorial and most intolerant of all the forms of government should have developed under modern conditions and on such a scale that it even threatens to engulf modern civilization? To put the answer in the shortest way, it is because under modern conditions the price of the abuse of power is far heavier than it ever was before. Dictatorship is the modern nemesis of prior misrule, of the miscalculations and follies of prior power systems. Before dictatorship appeared democracy had been making advances everywhere. It influenced the peoples which were subject to autocratic rule. It increased their restiveness and their sense of injustice. The new means of communication developed under democratic conditions brought to these peoples the doctrines and questionings of the new age. Suddenly autocratic misrule was intolerably aggravated by the outbreak of a world war. In their new misery and hopeless insecurity the misruled peoples were ready for revolt. But the ensuing chaos was most unfavorable for the difficult transition from oligarchy to democracy. So the dictators came, with their attendant cliques, and promised a new world, a world to be brought into being all at once, without the birth pangs of democracy. They won enough support from the disoriented and the desperate, from the frustrated and the oppressed, to seize the reins of power, an art they had carefully studied. Once in power, they could secure themselves only by stifling all opposition, for they possessed none of the "legitimacy" of the old monarchies and dynasties, and thus they knew that the slightest murmur of overt dissent from their claim to infallibility would expose their weakness and be the beginning of the end.

Index